Forty Quarts of Liquor
Fatty Arbuckle and the Death of Virginia Rappe

Contemporaneous accounts of
Hollywood's First Scandal

Edited by:
Dave Zuda

Forty Quarts of Liquor: Fatty Arbuckle and the Death of Virginia Rappe, Hollywood's First Scandal
Copyright 2018 Dave Zuda
2nd Edition

All rights reserved. No part of this book may be used or reproduced in any form or by any means without prior written permission except in the case of brief quotations embodied in critical articles and reviews.

ISBN-13: 978-1985236882
ISBN-10: 1985236885

facebook.com/BamberBooks

FOUR DAYS—STARTING TOMORROW

ROSCOE (Fatty) ARBUCKLE
—IN—
"The Life of The Party"

By Irwin S. Cobb.

A Paramount Picture.

The greatest five-reel comedy ever made! This comedy has been procured by special arrangement for Rialto patrons! Come—and laugh until you ache! This picture makes all other Arbuckle comedies look like rehearsals!

IT STARTS TOMORROW!

RIALTO

Introduction

It would be difficult to overstate the box office king that was Roscoe "Fatty" Arbuckle. Second only to Charlie Chaplin in receipts, Fatty made tons (*ha ha!*) of money for the studios; he also had a keen eye for the comedic arts, reportedly discovering Buster Keaton and, years later, Bob Hope, as well.

But it would be his eye for fetching young women that would be the undoing of the rotund funny man with the *million dollar smile*.

Nicknamed the *Life of the Party*, Arbuckle hosted a private revel in a suite of hotel rooms Labor Day weekend in 1921. The reader must understand this was the era of both Prohibition and the so-called Jazz-Baby. A devil-may-care time, albeit, but one in which a great many Americans were still rather puritanical.

Forty quarts of liquor were consumed by a handful of guests, one of whom, an attractive young actress named Virginia Rappe, died, allegedly under the weight of Fatty's 266 pounds. Rappe was found nude, with Fatty nearby in his bathrobe wearing the girl's hat.

What followed was a trial that gripped all of America as well as film fans across the globe. It was the O.J. trial of its time.

Here, your faithful editor has collected many contemporaneous (*i.e.*, newspaper reports and journal articles of the period) tellings of the first Hollywood scandal as the details emerged; readers will encounter them in bits just as did those riveted to the drama nearly 100 years ago.

–DZ

The Players

Some requisite background on both Fatty Arbuckle and Virginia Rappe is appropriate.

Arbuckle, of course, was a popular film comedian but his background, especially his strict upbringing, is relevant.

Miss Rappe would later be accused of promiscuity, though after reading her own words here, one would be hard-pressed to see her as anything but virtuous.

Emphasis and annotation are the editor's.

[*The Washington Times*, September 18, 1921]

Noted Psychologist Would Sentence "Fatty" Arbuckle to a Health Farm for Reduction of His Excess Tissue

Comedian's Rise from Bar Boy Is Closely Analyzed

How People and Facts In Life History of Man With Million-Dollar Smile May Have Been Allied With Avoirdupois According To Resume of Conditions That Would Enter Into Famous French Scientist's Analysis Of The Fatal Revel In San Francisco.

Andre Tridon, the Paris psychoanalyst whose fame has girdled the globe, has thus diagnosed the Arbuckle "complex:"

"If Roscoe Arbuckle committed the crime with which he is charged, he did it because he is fat!

"The hundred too many pounds rolling over the film comedian's body is so much moral weakness and potential crime.

"If he is found guilty the judge should sentence him not to prison, but to a gymnasium to lose fat.

"Accordingly, I believe Arbuckle should be tried by a jury of 12 psychologists and psychoanalysts, and that if he is found guilty he should be sentenced to a health farm or gymnasium to work off a hundred or more pounds."

Is the psychoanalyst right in his diagnosis of the situation that has resulted from the last exploit of Fatty Arbuckle, the man who for almost a decade has rejoiced in the title of being "the life of the party" – and whose great ambition in life was to give parties of which he could be the "life" – whether these parties were given in darkened movie palaces where the silver screen reflected his image to laughing tens of thousands or for a selected group of "bohemian" companions in a hotel suite, a California bungalow, or the comedian's Los Angeles resident?

Just how far does the condition in which the famous screen star finds himself bear out the psychoanalyst's diagnosis? What produces this condition in this particular case? What is the case?

Many and various versions of the Arbuckle affair have been unearthed by the District Attorney at San Francisco, his associates, and the friends of Miss Virginia Rappe, whose death was the third reel climax of this story.

Woman's description

There is first a woman writer's description of the man himself as he appears today – bare words through which she pictures the soul of the fat comedian. She writes:

"The great face, sickly hued and with dark circled eyes, still bore that paradoxical look – the asset which has lured a steady stream of gold. He looked at a great big bulking baby roused suddenly and rudely from sleep, its mind still bound by the thrall of another world. Searching its surroundings would show an uncertain hand, a familiar touch."

How many picture enthusiasts will recognize that word portrait?

How many times has that same sickly, almost idiotic, shape shown forth in a "close-up" on the screen when the comedian was supposed to "register" dismay? One can almost see the mouth over the tongue slowly and

Frequent life of the party "Fatty" Arbuckle surrounded by a bevy of beauties.

twitchingly lick the puppy lips? Then, it was almost succeeded by a sudden change to the "million dollar" smile. But now – read:

"Like a mist on a familiar landscape, apathy is slowly settling on 'Fatty' Arbuckle's face. He routs it for a moment by the sheer insistence of the mummer's training, but the alert muscular response is belied by the haggard eyes that, in the last few days, have looked deep into the mystery of his own heart and found – what?"

That is the subject presented today for analysis.

How did he get that way? What brought it about? In other words – how did the fat start to accumulate on the body, the mind and the purse?

Started on farm

Roscoe Arbuckle started life on an obscure farm in Kansas. He was a fat boy. A loving mother – later a stepmother – and a father who used the rod almost to the point of brutality – gave him what they could out of this slender store their meager acres allowed them to win. It was the typical small farm of the Middle West and the typical small farm family.

The advantages of schooling were only those afforded by such a district and the opportunity for that greater education – contact with the world and its interlocking emotions and activities were even more limited. Occasionally the farm boy went to the small village that was the source of supply for all things both material and spiritual that made for the "life" of the farm. The baby Roscoe was fat. The boy Roscoe was fat. The mother wanted her son to be a minister of the gospel. But the mother died.

The father planned to make him a country doctor.

And then – then one day there came to town a one ring circus.

The bewildering, clumsy, slapstick "art" of the clown gave to the fat farm boy the first gleam of real ambition that had penetrated to his barren image of life. For months, he cherished the dream this awkward, crude comedian inspired. He would be a clown!

One day, a regular tank town minstrel show played the village. Roscoe trudged to town and hung over the gallery rail drinking in every word of the raw humor handed out by these crude blackface comedians. That was the climax. That minstrel show pointed the road for "Fatty" Arbuckle. He was in his middle teens when a particularly savage beating decided him. He ran away from the farm and its lack of chance to do the things he wanted to do and sped towards the west. He worked his way to California doing odd jobs on the way and finally becoming the custodian of cuspidors of a cheap San Francisco saloon – ever watching for the chance to get on the stage, to become a real actor. Trials he had, but he failed.

Finally, he managed to hit a "rep" show that needed "actors." A "rep" show is a strange assortment of people and plays. It is a dramatic makeshift. It has makeshift plays, makeshift scenery and makeshift actors. It merely approximates the "drama" — and it plays those small towns and villages that boast of town halls and "opry" houses — <u>centers that merely approximate civilization</u> for the truly rural sections.

There are two general classes of amusement purveyors of this kind. One of them is the "rep" show and the other is the "Tom" show. The "Tom" show is called so from the fact that it produces what passes for "Uncle Tom's Cabin" among people who know nothing about Harriet Beecher Stowe's classic.

His first show

The company that Roscoe Arbuckle joined with was a combination "rep" and "Tom" outfit — it played both types. It played everything and anything. A very careful observer could pick out familiar situations of dozens of standard dramas in any one of its plays with strange high-sounding titles. Roscoe was a roustabout with the show.

His first attempt with it brought him a real serious part — and an influence that really had much to do with making for him what little success he enjoyed.

The audience laughed at his attempts to be an "actor." The manager tore his hair. But there was one member of the company — more farseeing than the manager or the audience — who recognized in this fat young man the same thing that everybody recognizes when a dignified person is spread-eagled by a banana peeling — the elemental inspiration of laughter. The round, moon shaped, vacant countenance shone for the first time on a person who appreciated its value.

The name of this wise player was Minta Durfee — she was an actress of fairly good roles because she was a real actress in a wise woman. She saw the possibilities in

"Fatty" Arbuckle. And she was possibly attracted by what appeared to be the utter incapability of fat to do anything of itself but be fat. She coached him. She MARRIED him finally and kept up constant coaching.

Fatty and Minta Durfee Arbuckle drifted all over California in rep and Tom shows and in vaudeville. They sped in circled about the larger centers, particularly Los Angeles.

Motion pictures were being made in Los Angeles. The vacant stare of Mack Sennett was making people laugh. The heavy, crude humor of Fred Mace was making them guffaw – the funny falls and plastic face of Ford Sterling made audiences howl.

To Minta – and to Fatty, through Minta's inspiration and constant urging – came the idea that Roscoe had the capacity for showing vacant countenance far beyond the ability of Mack Sennett, a heavier, bulkier personality than Fred Mace and a faculty of taking far more dangerous looking falls than Ford Sterling.

Picture star is born

And so, one day when Mack Sennett was looking for a particularly fat man to play the part of a Keystone policeman on whom the other acrobatic Keystone policemen could fall and tumble, he spied the bulk of Fatty Arbuckle among the hordes waiting to be hired as extras. And the Fatty Arbuckle of pictures commenced his career!

From the fat policeman with the round, moon, baby face that inspired shrieks of laughter, Fatty became a fixture in films. Sennett held onto Fatty and Minta kept up her course of instruction. Fatty became the idol of the Keystoners. Sennett found that the fat Roscoe was particularly effective with that diminutive little comedienne who meant so much to the early days of the Keystoners – Mabel Normand. And the "Fatty and Mabel" films were started that sent a gale of laughter echoing around the world.

Then came the scramble for screen stars – stars that brought money into the box office. Producers were beating for their services. The canny Mack Sennett kept a tight hold on the purse strings as long as he could, but the quotations on the grin that was visible when the moon face of Arbuckle was opened mounted higher and higher until it actually became a "million-dollar" smile.

"Fatty and Mabel" became the chief assets of a long-pursed producer. When Mabel Normand was injured and went through a long siege of ill health, "Fatty" started out on his own. He has been going on his own ever since. And his films have been among the best money getters in the business.

It was at the beginning of the time when the money commenced to flow into Arbuckle's treasure chest that <u>"Fatty" commenced to show his skill for being "the life of the party."</u> Just as the chubby baby wakes in its crib and gropes blindly for something – anything – so Fatty woke to the sunshine of life and groping found amusement in parties.

The constant stream of gold poured into the box offices by the laughter-seeking public brought a backwash as steady as the tides themselves into the purse of Fatty Arbuckle. Producers found that <u>the contrast of fun makers with the prettiest of girls</u> helped make for greater laughter and the pretty girls who wanted jobs – good paying jobs they were – with the film comedian sought entrance through working innocently enough, their feminine wiles on the comedian.

Given an unending supply of money and the constantly adoring public, together with the stream of the prettiest and dainty as the femininity all eager to please him, the grown-up child that was Fatty Arbuckle felt he was a "regular fellow."

He was the "life of the party" everywhere. Managers anxious to propitiate a star that brought them steadily increasing gains from an amusement-hungry public, and girls, eager to establish themselves in the film world, formed a very effective insulation against any other influence that might reach the fat comedian – and the fat, the fat of body, of mind and of purse continued to accumulate. The wife ceased to be the mentor. The comedian was made. And the business of the "the life of the party" sadly cut into such time as might have been given to domestic affairs. So Minta and Fatty were estranged. And they parted. But – that is another part of this story.

And with this situation grew up another. "Pathe" Lehrman, who had some ideas of dramatic production and particularly of comedy. He was a keen-minded director, and he needed the job of director. He started Fatty on his career in the Sennett Studios.

He, like Minta, recognized the raw material that a man of his caliber could make Fatty. He was a keen-minded analyst, too. He knew just what Fatty's possibilities were, and, as the director, he sought to bring as good acting as he could into the support of the comedian.

It was and is to be the interest of directors like Lehrman to keep on good terms with their stars. Into the Arbuckle entourage, Lehrman introduced many beautiful women – he wanted them as part of his pictures as contrasts for his star. And among them was Virginia Rappe. A girl of excellent instincts, a beauty who had her way to make and a woman who had a keen mind and a very sound understanding of the facts of life led by many of the people with whom she was associated in the film world, she walked with open eyes in this world.

There is the situation that the psychoanalysts see before them – upon which they start their diagnosis of the comedian. What are the stories that the witnesses of the various phases of this particular Fatty life tell, which, stripped of inaccuracies and the angularities of special viewpoints, will give the real facts?

First comes the stepmother, who took the place of his own mother when she passed away.

"He never had an education. He never passed the fifth grade school," declares this woman who knew the early life history. "His father mistreated him, I interfered and saved him from what I believe would have been a fatal beating at the hands of his father.

"I cannot help but pity the poor boy. It was his money that did it. Too much money went to his head."

And the paper which printed this statement of the stepmother closed its story by reciting that, "Mrs. Arbuckle, the little mother of two blind daughters, paused in her work of washing clothes for the best families of San Jose to tell of the early life of the film star!"

What does Minta Durfee Arbuckle say? Minta, the girl who "discovered" Fatty during those "rep" show days; the keen feminine instructructress who taught him all he knew; the wife who became excess baggage and was formally separated from her fat husband.

Read again:

"He is in great trouble. He must need me. I am going to him. That is all."

This is the greatest of Minta's reactions to the new phase of Fatty's life. And she – who KNOWS the man – declares:

"I am sure that all this is a frightful error and that my husband is innocent victim. He is not and never was such a man as is described in the charges. Others may think what they will – but I know."

Then there is another angle – a man's this time, Lehrman, the director, the friend and fiancé of Virginia Rappe, the man who declares that Arbuckle must answer to him. This is what Lehrman has to say:

"<u>This is what comes of taking vulgarians from the gutter and giving them enormous salaries and making idols of them</u>. Arbuckle came into the pictures nine years ago. He was a bar boy in a San Francisco saloon. He washed the dishes and cleaned the spittoons.

"Such people don't know how to get a 'kick' out of life except in a beastly way."

And then again he says:

"I excuse Miss Virginia Rappe's going to 'Fatty' Arbuckle's apartments in the San Francisco hotel, because she was in a strange town and lonesome.

"Miss Rappe was escorted by Mrs. Bambina Delmont, who has stated Virginia did not know Arbuckle was to be in the apartment when they were invited to call.

"Even if she had known Arbuckle was to be present I would've excused her going. For despite her physical aversion to him, he could have been entertaining."

Another man comes to the fore – a motion picture director also, who knew "Fatty." This director's name is Marshall Neilan. He is bitter against the public for its excoriation of Arbuckle. He says:

"It was the public that made 'Fatty.' It was the public that handed him its money, and I wish the public had stood by him at least until he was proved guilty. If Arbuckle committed the crime with which he is charged, <u>it</u>

was the fault of bad liquor and prohibition laws are to blame for bad liquor."

And then Neilan, as the friend of Arbuckle has this to say:

"I have known Fatty since the early days when he was in vaudeville. He was the kindest man in the world. He wouldn't have harmed the fly. Bad liquor was indeed to blame if he is guilty and as far as I can see the only thing against him is the testimony of others who had been drinking the same liquor."

What did Virginia think of Arbuckle? The witnesses who have been examined by the District Attorney of San Francisco seem to agree that the girl accused Arbuckle of having hurt her.

What this had to do with her death the juries will have to find out. And that is all anybody knows from the girl's own lips about the Arbuckle party directly. But what is her outlook on the sort of life and the sort of parties of which Arbuckle was "the life" so many times?

In an interview with the newspaper in Chicago regarding the "jazz baby" type of girl, Miss Rappe is reported to have said this:

The Washington Times *then quotes from the following article, which is inserted here in its entirety:*

[*Evening Public Ledger*, September 14, 1921]
Miss Rappe Told Girls of Pitfalls
Victim's Final Advice to Her Sex Warned Against Too Much Liberty
"Lead the Quiet Life"

(Chicago, Sept. 14.) Virginia Rappe's last advice to the girls of America, given in a newspaper interview, was summed up in these words:

"Lead the quiet life."

The interview was printed here under Miss Rappe's signature as follows:

"To be real frank, this entire discussion, which amounts to nothing more than whether or not a girl's enjoyment shall be curtailed was brought about through the mistake of the girls. A privilege was abused. And now amends are to be made.

"There is an old saying – Mr. Lehrman made use of it in his comedy *A Twilight Baby* – 'You can give a cow enough rope.' It's the same with girls. Give them enough rope and they won't know when to stop dancing, go home or anything else.

"The foregoing is a radical view, some of the aggrieved girls may say. And yet there are just as many girls who will agree that they didn't appreciate their liberty, and consequently overstepped the bounds.

"There is one way of meeting the problem on a fair basis, and that is through arbitration. And the girls must take the first step towards the halfway line.

"Hardly a city in this land hasn't a young set that consistently comes autoing home at all hours of the morning.

The mothers know this. <u>For a while, especially during the war, when the men in khaki had to be entertained, they tolerated it.</u> Now they're determined to stop it.

"There isn't a girl of fair dancing ability who hasn't been forced to be civil to <u>the insipid lounge lizard class that persists in haunting dance halls and clubs.</u> Personally, I don't know why the lounge lizard exists. Even the cootie, the fly and the ant have a mission in life— but the lounge lizard – I can't explain it.

"The mothers appreciate this. They want to break the association and break it right now! I don't blame them.

"Where did the 'jazz baby' idea originate? At the dances, midnight dances, all my dances. Any sane girl knows

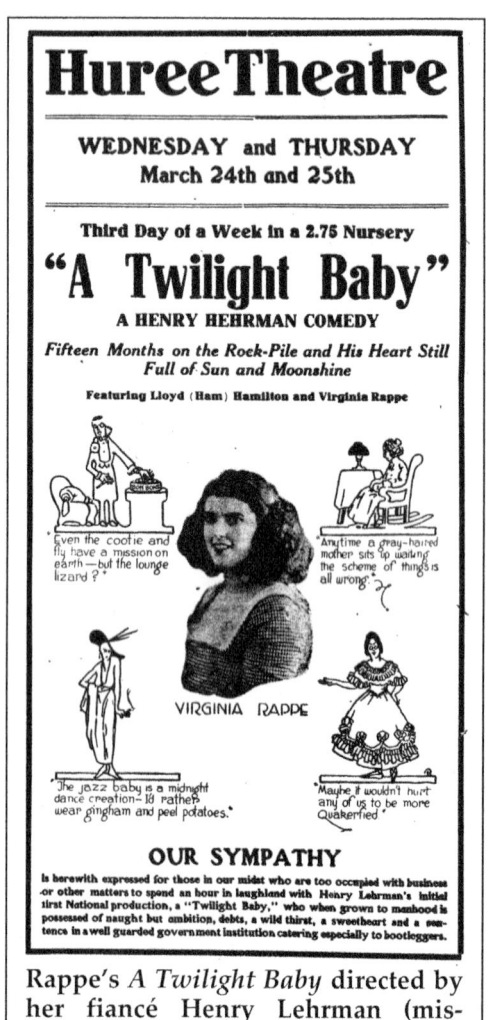

> **Huree Theatre**
>
> WEDNESDAY and THURSDAY
> March 24th and 25th
>
> Third Day of a Week in a 2.75 Nursery
>
> **"A Twilight Baby"**
> A HENRY HEHRMAN COMEDY
>
> *Fifteen Months on the Rock-Pile and His Heart Still Full of Sun and Moonshine*
>
> Featuring Lloyd (Ham) Hamilton and Virginia Rappe
>
> "Even the cootie and fly have a mission on earth—but the lounge lizard?"
>
> "Anytime a gray-haired mother sits up waiting the scheme of things is all wrong."
>
> VIRGINIA RAPPE
>
> "The jazz baby is a midnight dance creation– I'd rather wear gingham and peel potatoes."
>
> "Maybe it wouldn't hurt any of us to be more Quakerfied."
>
> **OUR SYMPATHY**
>
> Is herewith expressed for those in our midst who are too occupied with business or other matters to spend an hour in laughland with Henry Lehrman's initial first National production, a "Twilight Baby," who when grown to manhood is possessed of naught but ambition, debts, a wild thirst, a sweetheart and a sentence in a well guarded government institution catering especially to bootleggers.
>
> Rappe's *A Twilight Baby* directed by her fiancé Henry Lehrman (misspelled above). Rappe lived with Lehrman just before she died.

'jazz baby' ideas are all wrong.

"While we were making *A Twilight Baby* and I was in the barnyard scene, a party of tourists came to visit Mr. Lehrman's studio.

"One of the boys whispered to me that a young girl onlooker was a typical 'jazz baby.' I told him I'd rather be the girl in gingham and peel potatoes. And I meant it. The mothers know this and want to keep their daughters out of the 'jazz baby' element. Who can blame them?

"I think the girl's dates should bring as much pleasure to the mother as to the girl herself. Any time a girl decides to have an evening's entertainment against the wishes of the mother or leaves the mother waiting-up for her return, the scheme of things is all wrong.

"After thinking over the problem, is it hard to see that concessions must be made? After all, a mother's wish is about the best thing for everybody concerned.

"And perhaps it wouldn't hurt any of us to be a little more like Quakerfield[1]!"

Resuming to the Washington Times *piece:*

What sort of girl was Virginia Rappe – the girl who gave the advice that has been quoted for the government of the conduct of girls generally?

Here is what her closest friend, Mrs. Joseph Hardebeck, said of her:

"Virginia was a sweet, kindly girl – as nice a girl as could be found. She had few men friends and she wasn't intimate with many girls.

"For the last few months, Virginia stayed home almost constantly. Her chief delight was in tramping over

---

[1] Unknown reference.

the hills over Hollywood with her dog. I don't think she went out with other people more than two or three times in the last six weeks.

"She knew Arbuckle. But she knew him just as she knew all the other boys and girls at the motion picture colony. So far as I know, he was never in her house and she was never in his.

"She knew Arbuckle," this friend of the dead girl states. How well did she know him? This is her description of him given to her fiancé, Lehrman, on another occasion:

"He's course and vulgar! He nauseates me! He is cheap and he thinks he's funny!"

She said this of the man who was the "life of the party" at the St. Francis Hotel – to which she was summoned by telephone and from which she was carried to the hospital where she died, declaring:

"Roscoe did this. Make him pay for it."

And there you have the whole situation.

The punishment the psychologists would mete-out would send the victim to a health farm where exercise, fresh air and no alcohol would reduce the amount of – fat!

Additional background.

[*Albuquerque Morning Journal*, September 13, 1921]

Fatty Was Popular Among the Children

(San Jose, Calif., Sept. 12.) Roscoe C. (Fatty) Arbuckle, under arrest in San Francisco under a murder charge, played the part of the "Pied Piper" to the children of Santa Clara, near here, according to a statement today by his stepmother, Mrs. Molly Arbuckle. Mrs. Arbuckle is a washerwoman and charwoman. Her husband died four years ago.

"He was so big and good-natured and so full of fun that the children used to follow him around to watch his antics," she said. "He was always good-humored.

"He got his start in San Jose by singing in the theaters. Then he went away, years ago, and I did not hear from him until about five years ago when he appeared in a San Jose theater. I spoke to him for a few minutes then.

"Roscoe was always kind to me but he never offered to support me and I never expected him to. I do not feel it was his place to support me.

"If he is innocent I want to see him cleared. If he is guilty I want to see him punished to the limit."

According to Mrs. Arbuckle, Roscoe Arbuckle is an uncle of Al St. John, motion picture actor of Los Angeles. He has a brother, Arthur Arbuckle, in San Francisco, and another brother, Harry Arbuckle, in Fresno, she said.

Her husband was a hard-working man but sometimes lost his temper, she said, and during one of these bits of temper, <u>he beat Roscoe severely</u>.

[*Evening Public Ledger*, September 14, 1921]
Remembered Arbuckle as mischievous lad
(Smith Center, Kan., Sept. 14.) Residents of this county remember "Fatty" Arbuckle as a fat, overgrown lad, always seeking and getting into mischief, but never given to cruelty or violence. His natural bent seemed to be towards acting on the stage, and he was never happier, even in boyhood, than when entertaining his friends with clownish performances.

Of humble parentage, "Fatty" was born in a sod house in the northeast section of this county in 1887, and all his early surroundings were of the rough, primitive sort.

His parents had a hard time making a living on the farm, and a few years after "Fatty's" birth, they moved to the city. The lad always attracted attention by his size and roguish disposition and his readiness to make friends with everybody.

In school, he was quick to learn, but his teachers constantly were on the alert to prevent the execution of his pranks. From this city the Arbuckle family moved to Santa Ana, Calif., when "Fatty" was about 10 years old.

[*Washington Times*, September 20, 1921]
Daughter of nobleman
Virginia Rappe, who died following injuries received at "Fatty's" party, was the daughter of an English nobleman, according to the story told today by Mrs. Joseph Rafferty, and intimate friend of Virginia's grandmother.

Her mother, Mable Rappe, was jilted by the Englishman during the Chicago World's Fair after she had given up the chance to wed a wealthy Chicago man.

Mable Rappe was a beauty. Foreign visitors were infatuated with her. She was even more beautiful than Virginia. Mrs. Rafferty's story follows:

"Contrary to report, Virginia was born in New York instead of Chicago.

"My knowledge of Virginia's parentage is based upon information given me by her grandmother. I was then a nurse, one well acquainted with the grandmother and a friend of Virginia, then a girl of about 16. This was in 1910.

"According to the grandmother's story, Mabel Rappe met many of the foreign visitors to the World's Fair, among them a titled Englishman. At the time, she was engaged to a wealthy young man. Her relations with the Englishman became so open that the engagement was broken off.

"She then announced her engagement to the Englishman who sailed for home at the close of the Fair, promising to return to marry Mable. Mable left for New York, where Virginia was born, and where her mother remained until her death.

"Mable Rappe remained in New York eight years. Her death was due to an affliction of the throat.

"Virginia had been attending a private school there, and at the death of her mother, Virginia's grandmother sent for the child and brought her to Chicago. Developing early into a strikingly beautiful girl, Virginia, after finishing school, readily obtained employment as a model and helped support herself and her grandmother."

Pantalets of '50 Are Back Again
Chicago Girls Wear 'Em on Liner

Virginia Rappe.

Before coming to Hollywood, Virginia Rappe was a model in Chicago. From *The Chicago Examiner*, January 12, 1914.

It begins

Probably because of the effectiveness of the Hollywood hush machine, little was reported between the time of Rappe's injury (Monday, September 5th) and her death four days later (Friday afternoon, September 9th). But when news broke of her demise, it spread as fast as the investigation escalated and Arbuckle's arrest was swift.

[*Carson City Daily Appeal*, September 10, 1921]

Death of Actress Causes Investigation
Fatty Arbuckle called on to help explain cause

(San Francisco, Sept. 10.) Roscoe (Fatty) Arbuckle, with his attorney, Frank Dominquez, is expected here this afternoon to confer with the police regarding the death of Miss Virginia Rappe, a movie actress, following a party alleged to have been given in Arbuckle's hotel room here last Monday.

Arbuckle left Los Angeles by automobile early today.

The police quoted Arbuckle as saying that after a few drinks Miss Rappe became hysterical and he summoned the hotel manager and had her removed to another room.

Physicians were summoned, but the girl died yesterday.

The attending doctors, it is alleged, performed an autopsy before the coroner's permit was secured.

[*Daily Times*, September 10, 1921]
Fatty Arbuckle in Trouble
Connected With the Death of Motion Picture Actress Who Died In His Hotel

(San Francisco, Calif., Sept. 10.) Following the death of Miss Virginia Rappe, a motion picture actress, in a section of a Los Angeles[2] hotel occupied by Roscoe (Fatty Arbuckle), that actor left for San Francisco today with his attorney stating that he would assist the authorities in arriving at the cause of her death.

An autopsy of the body of the woman by a local chemist showed that she died of congestion of the lungs induced by peritonitis of the stomach.

As the result of a party in the rooms of Arbuckle in Los Angeles, Arbuckle was asked to leave the hotel by the proprietor. Arbuckle claims that Miss Rappe came to his room after she had taken two drinks and was taken ill and that two other women callers took her to another room and looked after her. A physician was called.

He claimed that he did not know anything about the seriousness of her condition until after he learned that she was dead.

---

[2] A reporting error.

[*Capital Journal*, September 10, 1921]
Roscoe Arbuckle Held by Police
Girl Friend Dead
Police investigation shows Virginia Rappe died following party in actor's rooms; women say girl found with "Fatty" nearly nude and partly unconscious

(San Francisco September 10.) Roscoe (Fatty) Arbuckle, motion picture actor, is to be "held in custody" pending the outcome of the police investigation into the death of Miss Virginia Rappe, following a party in Arbuckle's room at the St. Francis Hotel here, acting Captain of Detectives Michael Griffith announced today.

"Arbuckle will not be arrested," Griffith said, "but he will be detained by us until the investigation has been concluded. I have put four detectives on the case. I understand that he is coming up here voluntarily but he will be compelled to remain until the police are finished with him. At present we are not contemplating any charge against him."

Grand jury to probe

The County grand jury is to start an investigation Monday into Miss Rappe's death and Arbuckle's interest in it, Harry Kelly, secretary of the jury said today.

"So many women's clubs and private individuals interested in the moral welfare of the city have demanded an investigation that I will present their demands to the jury," Kelly said. "It is our duty to investigate such things and we will certainly do so. The District Attorney who is now out of the city will be advised of the circumstances and he will handle the matter before the grand jury."

Autopsy is held

Dr. R. M. Rumwell, who attended Miss Rappe in the hotel following the party, and Dr. Wm. Oppolus, who performed an autopsy on her, were called to the coroner's office to be questioned concerning their knowledge of the case.

The party was held last Monday afternoon. Hotel authorities said they requested Arbuckle to leave as a result of the affair, which he did.

According to Detective Kennedy, a man who said he was Arbuckle telephoned from Los Angeles to the detective bureau at 11 o'clock last night and said he would return here today to assist the police in every way possible in clearing up the Rappe case.

The police are not considering bringing any charge at present against anybody involved in the death of Miss Rappe, Kennedy said, but future developments might change the situation, however.

Murder charge pends

"The only charge that could be suggested by cases of this character is murder," Kennedy said, "and we have no evidence as yet that such a charge is justified. However the situation is an extremely serious one."

Kennedy said he would question all of those who attended the party.

According to women members of the party, Arbuckle and Miss Rappe went into one of the rooms of the hotel suite and the door of the room was thereupon locked. Later there were cries and <u>sounds of a scuffle</u> in the room, they said, and they pounded on the door for admittance. Arbuckle finally admitted them, they said, and they saw Miss Rappe on a bed, practically nude and but partially conscious. <u>Her clothing was badly torn, they said, even to her stockings</u>.

She was placed in a cold bath in an endeavor to revive her, but this had no effect and she was taken into another room and put to bed. The house physician was called and later she was taken to the sanitarium where she died.

Arbuckle denies story

Arbuckle in his conversation with the police last night, specifically denied all of the statements made by the other members of the party, saying that he was not alone with Miss Rappe at any time and that his conduct at no time was objectionable.

[*Lake County Times*, September 10, 1921]

"Fatty" Arbuckle Is Gravely Accused
Found Lightly Clad In Hotel Room with Girl Who Later Dies at the Hospital

(San Francisco, Sept. 10.) "Fatty" Arbuckle, film comedian and host of a gay party at the St. Francis Hotel here last Monday, expected by police to arrive here today from Los Angeles to give his version of the events leading up to the sudden illness which [*unintelligible*] Miss Virginia Rappe, beautiful young movie actress, in the midst of the party, which resulted in her death here late yesterday.

According to the hotel management, Arbuckle, with Fred Fishback, and L. Sherman, of Los Angeles, occupied a suite of rooms. A request came about noon last Monday that a phonograph be sent to the suite. This was complied with on condition there be no dancing. Later a call came from the rooms for assistance stating a woman in the party had become ill.

Assistant manager H. J. Boyle responded and found Miss Rappe lying on a bed lightly clad and unconscious. Arbuckle was clad in pajamas in a bathrobe, it was stated, explaining that his friends had called while he was having breakfast in his room.

Miss Rappe was removed to a hospital the next day and several other physicians were called in consultation. Medical science was of no avail and death came late yesterday after she was found to be in a serious condition.

Arbuckle's mug shot.

Fallout

As in the 2017 celebrity scandals that produced the #meetoo and #timesup movements, public reaction to the fallen clown was quick and practically everyone moved to distance themselves from the accused.

[*Capital Journal*, September 12, 1921]
Pictures by Arbuckle on black lists

Despite the fact that prominent city officials of Salem have expressed themselves as favoring the suspension from local screens those motion pictures in which Roscoe "Fatty" Arbuckle, comedian who is charged with murder, appears, no formal action can be taken to ban the pictures from Salem, according to city attorney Ray Smith.

In Salem, an ordinance names the mayor, the chief of police and the police matron as a censorship committee, but the same ordinance specifies the type of picture which shall be considered objectionable. It shall be immoral or obscene before any action may be taken by the censors.

Charles Kupper, manager of the Oregon Theater, stated this morning he "didn't know whether or not

Arbuckle pictures would be shown here," when asked if he would take action similar to that of certain other theater managers.

(Los Angeles, Sept. 12.) The latest film production featuring Roscoe "Fatty" Arbuckle, held in jail in San Francisco in connection with the death of Miss Virginia Rappe, was canceled last night at one of the largest local motion picture houses. The film had been showing all last week, and last night's was to have been its final appearance.

(Medford, Mass., Sept. 12.) Mayor Haines today notified all motion picture houses here that films of Roscoe (Fatty) Arbuckle, the screen star held in San Francisco in connection with the death of Miss Virginia Rappe, would be barred until Arbuckle's case has been disposed of in the courts.

(Memphis, Tenn., Sept 12.) The Memphis Board of Censors announced today that the showing of motion pictures featuring Roscoe (Fatty) Arbuckle would not be permitted in Memphis theaters until he had cleared himself of the charges against him in connection with the death of Miss Virginia Rappe in San Francisco.

(Detroit, Mich., Sept. 12.) All pictures featuring Roscoe Arbuckle were placed under ban today by the Michigan Motion Picture Exhibitors Association, until the case against the film comedian is disposed of.

(Ogden, Utah, Sept. 12.) H. E. Skinner, manager of Ogden's largest photoplay theater, announced today he had canceled three Arbuckle films because of the notoriety attending the San Francisco episode.

[*The Seattle Star*, September 17, 1921]
Fatty's Film Burned by Mob; 25 Cops Handle Throng
(Thermopolis, Wyoming Sept. 27.) Hundreds of persons formed a mob here last night, attacked a motion picture theater, seized a film portraying Roscoe (Fatty) Arbuckle, and burned it in the streets. Police were unable to stop the demonstration.

Following an announcement by the theater proprietor that the Arbuckle film would be shown Friday night, protests were made by scores of citizens. Final efforts by a security squad to induce the management of the show to refrain from exhibiting the film following indictment of the comedian in San Francisco in connection with the death of Miss Virginia Rappe were unavailing.

When the show opened last night, the mob smashed into the lobby and into the operator's cage and threw the film to the street, where it was burned.

Other responses:

[*Washington Times*, September 20, 1921]
Chaplin happy as Paris demands Arbuckle films
(Paris, Sept. 20.) Charlie Chaplin showed his practical belief in the innocence of "Fatty" Arbuckle here.

Snatching a moment from his enjoyment of Montmartre night palaces and dodging his admirers, Charlie visited the Marivaux Theater, where the latest "Fatty" film to reach Paris was showing.

Later to friends, Charlie confided his satisfaction at the "unhysterical" attitude of the Parisian movies syndicate, which is not only <u>not refusing to show Arbuckle</u>

films, but is rushing orders for more in order to fill the sudden demand.

The comment of the Paris papers on the Arbuckle case is chiefly humorous. It is understood that Arbuckle will be offered a job in France should his career be ended in the United States.

[*Washington Times*, September 20, 1921]
Chicago may bar films until Arbuckle's trial
(Chicago, Sept. 20.) Pictures in which Roscoe Arbuckle, charged with the murder of Miss Virginia Rappe, motion picture actress, is a principal may be barred from Chicago until "Fatty" has proven his innocence of the charge against him.

A resolution asking Chief of Police Fitzmorris to take such action was yesterday adopted by the City Council and placed in the hands of the Chief of Police.

Arbuckle's high-profile incident brought scrutiny on the entire industry.

[*Capital Journal*, September 12, 1921]
Other parties in Los Angeles being probed
(Los Angeles, Sept. 12.) Reports of "parties" in which "drug and drink" figured and at which Roscoe (Fatty) Arbuckle, held in San Francisco in connection with the death of Miss Virginia Rappe, was said to have been present, are being investigated by the Los Angeles Morals Efficiency Commission, according to a statement by the

commission today through J. H. Pelletier, executive secretary.

One specific case under investigation was reported to have taken place recently at Hollywood according to the statement. Some of those present were alleged to have been under the influence of stimulants or narcotics was one of the reports declared to be under investigation.

[*Evening Public Ledger*, September 14, 1921]

Hollywood Orgies May Be Revealed

(Los Angeles, Sept. 14.) Drink and drug orgies here which have been reported to the Morals Efficiency Association may figure in the San Francisco inquiry into the Roscoe Arbuckle case. Captain J. E. Pelletier, of the Association and in the war as an officer of the United States Interdepartmental Bureau of Social Hygiene, declared that he was sending certain evidence to the District Attorney at San Francisco.

Investigators of the Morals Efficiency Association have made several reports now on file in Captain Pelletier's offices which bear on the situation. One such report describes a party in which 125 persons, including many wealthy men not connected with pictures, took part.

"After they drank booze and use drugs freely, men and women danced in the nude, according to my investigations," he declared.

"I have not found anyone with courage enough to appear in court, but several of those present have given me, privately, the details of the affair. When they learned I had the party under investigation they sent a woman here to pump me. She represented herself as a newspaper reporter, but she did not get away with it. It was too crude; she wanted to know how far it had gone."

Captain Pelletier declared he has located and stopped the supply of liquor and has found and soon will stop the source of drugs being supplied to the clique to which he refers.

Court drama unfolds

The bulk of Arbuckle activity occurred in the inquest and various grand jury deliberations, arraignments and three trials described herein. Emphasis and annotation are the editor's.

[*Capital Journal*, September 12, 1921]

Arbuckle Is Accused of Killing Girl
Film Comedian Held Without Bail on Charge Preferred by Friend of Dead Actress;

Prosecutor Says Case Against "Fatty" Complete;

Coroner's Inquest Today.

(San Francisco, Sept. 12.) A formal complaint charging murder was sworn to before police judge Daniel O'Brien today against the Roscoe C. (Fatty) Arbuckle in connection with the death of Miss Virginia Rappe, a motion picture actress. The complaint was signed by Mrs. Bambina Maude Delmont, a friend of the dead actress.

Arbuckle appeared in court to be arraigned on the charge sworn to by Mrs. Delmont. At the request of the District Attorney the case was continued until Friday morning and Arbuckle was taken back to his cell.

Dr. T. B. W. Leland, city and county coroner, said that the inquest would start today, but probably would not be concluded until tomorrow. Drs. Arthur Beardslee, William Ophuls and M. E. Rumwell who attended Miss Rappe, will be called on to testify today, he said. Arbuckle will be present at the inquest, but may not testify today.

In his answer to [*Rappe's fiancé*] Lehrman, Brady said Miss Rappe's body would not be shipped to her home in Los Angeles until after the inquest. He asked Lehrman what his wishes were in regard to the funeral.

Mrs. Delmont appeared to be near collapse after making the charge against Arbuckle.

The arrangement was conducted in a haze of flashlight smoke, the flashlights popping with machine-gun regularity.

Arbuckle appeared through a side door, flanked by his attorneys and the police guard. He appeared greatly dejected and heaved many sighs.

Courtroom packed

Following the court session and before he was taken back to his cell, he was given an opportunity to go to the judge's chambers and smoke a cigarette while the arraignment papers were being made out.

The little courtroom was packed, the spectators rising in their chairs when Arbuckle appeared and remaining in that position during the brief session. There were few women present.

District Attorney Brady announced that he had received a telegram from Henry Lehrman, motion picture producer of New York and fiancé of Miss Rappe, asking him to obtain a sworn statement from Mrs. Delmont. Brady replied that the statement had already been obtained.

Mrs. Spreckels named

Brady said also that he had sent for Mrs. Sidi Wirt Spreckels, widow of John D. Spreckels Jr.[3], who was killed in an automobile accident recently, to question her regarding a visit she made to Miss Rappe at the girl's request after the attack.

Mrs. Delmont, in signed and sworn statements, gave the police many details of the party in Arbuckle's rooms in the St. Francis Hotel here a week ago today, at which time Miss Rappe was subjected to an alleged attack by Arbuckle. She died four days later.

Mrs. Delmont attended the party and assisted Miss Rappe after the alleged attack. She appeared personally in court to swear to the complaint. Arbuckle was not in court when the complaint was filed.

Arbuckle is held without bail in the Hall of Justice here. He was arrested last Saturday night on his arrival from Los Angeles and was booked on a charge of murder.

Goes to grand jury

The Arbuckle case is scheduled to be brought before the San Francisco county grand jury tonight. A coroner's inquest into Miss Rappe's death has been called for next Thursday.

Arbuckle has requested that none but his attorneys be allowed to see him at the Hall of Justice. He declined yesterday, on the advice of counsel, to make any statement. His lawyers also refused to make a statement or discuss the case in any way.

Police yesterday were busy examining witnesses whom they say will be presented to the grand jury to-

---

[3] A volume could be written about the Spreckels family and the reader is encouraged to pursue the topic.

night. These witnesses number 22 and are being guarded by police detectives.

Eats big breakfast

Arbuckle went to bed on his narrow cell couch at 9 o'clock last night and apparently slept soundly. When the prison watch shouted "everybody up" at the usual rising time today, he awakened, but rolled over on the bed and tried to go to sleep again. He was told he must get up, however, so he arose, smilingly.

While he did not take advantage of the prison showers, he dressed with the greatest care. He ordered his breakfast from the outside and when the waiter came, held a long, secret conference with him.

The waiter brought back a carefully covered tray which Arbuckle attacked with all of the secrecy possible.

He continued to decline to see any visitors, other than his attorneys. He is scheduled to appear in police court for formal arraignment today.

Captain of Detectives Matheson ordered that Arbuckle be placed in the regular morning lineup of prisoners which is held for the police detectives each morning, and that he be photographed for the rogue's gallery and his fingerprints and Bertillon measurements taken.

Arbuckle consented later to see a group of newspaper men, but refused to discuss the Rappe case with them. He appeared dejected but said he was receiving good treatment in the jail.

District Attorney Brady through Deputy Milton T. U'Ren, said, "We have a complete case against Arbuckle."

Arbuckle's appearance in police court was delayed until his Bertillon measurements could be taken and he could be photographed for the rogue's gallery.

The measurements showed that his weight was 266 pounds and his height 5 feet 8 3/8 inches. He gave his birthplace as Kansas and his age at 34.

Lehrman to push charge

(New York, Sept. 12.) Henry Lehrman, motion picture director, who was engaged to marry Virginia Rappe, the film actress for whose death Roscoe Arbuckle is held in jail in San Francisco, today said he would devote every moment he could spare from his business to pressing the comedian's prosecution.

"I cannot get to the coast in person," he said, "but I am doing everything that can be done by telephone."

Mr. Lehrman said that he would supervise funeral arrangements after the inquest in San Francisco Thursday. Miss Rappe, he said, had no near relatives. Burial will be in Los Angeles.

[*Albuquerque Morning Journal*, September 13, 1921]

Murder Charge Lodged Against Fatty Arbuckle
Complaint Made by Mrs. Delmont In Connection With the Death of Miss Virginia Rappe, Actress

Accused Appears at Coroner's Inquest

Defendant's Attorney Asked Public to Withhold Judgment until the Court Has Rendered Its Verdict

(San Francisco, Sept. 12.) A formal charge of murder was filed in police court here today charging Roscoe C. (Fatty) Arbuckle, motion picture comedian, with murder[4] in connection with the death last Friday of Miss Virginia

---

[4] Refer to page 66 for a relevant discussion on the legal distinction between murder and manslaughter.

Rappe, motion picture actress. The charge, the second filed against Arbuckle since Friday night, was sworn to by Mrs. Bambina Maude Delmont, a friend of Miss Rappe, who attended a party in Arbuckle's suite in a hotel here a week ago today.

At the party, according to a witness, intoxicating liquors were consumed, and <u>Arbuckle, it is alleged by the District Attorney, attacked Miss Rappe</u>. The inquest into the death of the motion picture actress was started this afternoon by the county coroner.

Will plead Friday

Arbuckle appeared at the inquest and earlier in the day he had appeared in police court to be arraigned on the charge filed by Mrs. Delmont.

Pleading in the case was continued until Friday.

The film comedian was measured and photographed by the police for the rogue's gallery. He gave his age as 34. He weighed 266 pounds.

The grand jury was called tonight to consider the death of Miss Rappe. Her body will be sent to her former home in Los Angeles for interment after the inquest.

Before the inquest began, Arbuckle's attorneys, taking cognizance of the trend of public opinion as evidenced by the cancellation of the showings of pictures in which the comedian is the star, issued a statement <u>asking the public to withhold judgment until the court has rendered its verdict</u>. The statement said, in part:

"With a full knowledge of our position as attorneys, we assert that Roscoe (Fatty) Arbuckle is innocent of any and all charges made against him in connection with the death of Miss Virginia Rappe, and that the courts of California will sustain our confidence in his innocence.

"We appeal to the conscience and the heart of the American public to hold in abeyance any judgment until the courts have determined upon the guilt or innocence of our client. We, with complete knowledge of all facts, know that he is innocent.

"The patrons of the silent drama, having the knowledge of the smiles and the heart of Fatty Arbuckle, will not believe that he is guilty of the charge made against him until proven in a court of justice."

The manager of the Hotel St. Francis, where Arbuckle had his suite, was ordered today to appear before the district Federal Prohibition Enforcement officer to be questioned regarding the liquor said to have been consumed by the Arbuckle party.

Begs To Be Allowed To Remain In Cell

(San Francisco, Calif., Sept 12.) Unable to hide his deep concern under the mask of a faultless grooming of his dress and his person, Roscoe (Fatty) Arbuckle went into the police court today to hear that he was charged with the murder of Miss Virginia Rappe, film actress, and that he must stand trial. He tried to avoid the court ordeal, begging that he be allowed to remain in his cell and away from the throngs that he was told were pressing against the courtroom doors for a sight of him.

The quick changing grimaces and brisk actions, which brought laughter to millions and put Arbuckle on the pedestal of stardom, have gone from him. He had a serious downcast look. He was silent and smoked innumerable cigarettes throughout the day.

So long was the process of bringing Arbuckle into court delayed that Chief Judge Daniel S. O'Brien made a demand on Captain of Detectives Duncan Mathewson that the prisoner be produced without further delay.

"I have Arbuckle's case on the calendar," he said, "and he must be brought into the courtroom. He must accept the same treatment being accorded other prisoners."

Finally he came, after the motley array of usual police court cases had been disposed of. Down the packed corridors, silent under a heavy, morbid curiosity, he appeared haltingly, avoiding the eyes that peered at him from every angle. As he entered the courtroom through a side door, a battery of flashlights [*flashbulbs*] opened upon him, the popping of the flashlight guns having something of the staccato cadence of a machine gun battery. Arbuckle was unmindful of this, but when the court advised him that he would have to stand trial on a charge of murder, his head drooped, his hands trembled.

A few moments before, Mrs. Bambina Maud Delmont, companion of Arbuckle and his gay company in the party in a hotel here in which Miss Rappe, according to the authorities, received fatal injuries, had staggered from the courtroom after fixing her name to a bit of paper which said that Arbuckle was accused of murdering Miss Rappe, and which constituted the formal charge. But a few hours away from a sickbed where the tragedy that overwhelmed the party had sent her, she was weak and halting and hardly able for the ordeal.

[*Albuquerque Morning Journal*, September 13, 1921]

Probe Is Held Into Death of Movie Actress

Mrs. Spreckels Gives Vivid Account of the Last Hours of Miss Virginia Rappe in a Hotel Room

(San Francisco, Sept. 12.) Roscoe (Fatty) Arbuckle, who was the defendant in a police court murder arraignment this morning as dramatic as any motion picture, spent the afternoon at a coroner's inquest into the death of Miss Virginia Rappe, a film actress whose life he is charged with having taken.

Tonight he went back to his cell to await the outcome of a grand jury investigation in which Mrs. Bambina Maude Delmont, a member of the party in Arbuckle's hotel suite a week ago, from which the death of Miss Rappe ensued, was expected to be the leading witness.

She did not testify at the opening session of the inquest, the District Attorney saying that her appearance today previous to the grand jury session would handicap the authorities. Instead, the story was told by physicians and others of Miss Rappe's removal from Arbuckle suite, her treatment in another hotel room and later at a hospital, her death and the postmortem examination

Although his part in the affair was the central point of interest, Arbuckle was an almost unnoticed figure at the inquest, a sharp contrast to the arraignment, where a sea of faces banked the courtroom like a prize fight arena and a dozen petty law violators pressed unshaven faces against the steel grating of the prisoners' dock to a screen star performer without an admission charge.

The most vivid account of Miss Rappe's last hours was given before the inquest by Mrs. Sidi Wirt Spreckels, widow of John D. Spreckels Jr., who was called to the hospital last Friday morning, a few hours before the end. "To think that I have led such a quiet life and that I should've gotten into such a party," were among Rappe's last words, Mrs. Spreckels said in a formal statement to District Attorney Matthew A. Brady.

The party in Arbuckle's room appeared as the event from which Miss Rappe's death followed, but the physicians were unable to say at the inquest what was the exact cause of death.

Henry J. Boyle, assistant manager of the hotel, testified at the inquest that when called by Mrs. Delmont to Arbuckle's suite, he found Mrs. Delmont and Al Semnacher, who are said to have accompanied Miss Rappe to San Francisco from Los Angeles, sitting on the edge of the bed where Miss Rappe lay moaning and unconscious.

Arbuckle himself picked up Miss Rappe and carried her down the hotel corridor to another room, where she stayed until being taken to the hospital three days later, according to Boyle's testimony. At the door of this room, however, the film comedian's strength gave out, Boyle said, and Boyle had to complete the journey.

Boyle testified that Arbuckle and another member of the party told him Miss Rappe only had three drinks.

Too much liquor was the diagnosis given by Dr. Olav Kaarboe, the first physician called in, according to Kaarboe's own statement. At that time there was no evidence of serious injury, he said. Dr. M. E. Rumwell testified he was called into the case to succeed the second physician, Dr. Arthur Beardslee. He said Miss Rappe's condition did not seem serious until Thursday of last week, when a consultation was held.

Dr. Rumwell said there was nothing to indicate she had suffered from any violence until the postmortem examination, when he said evidence of internal injury was found.

At that point Dr. Rumwell made up his mind, he said, that this was a case which should be investigated by the corner and was about to notify the authorities when a deputy coroner appeared at the hospital.

Dr. William Ophuls, called into the case to perform the postmortem operation, described the internal injuries, but said he could not say definitely what caused them.

The inquest will be resumed tomorrow morning.

[*Evening Public Ledger*, September 14, 1921]
Manslaughter Indictment Placed Against Arbuckle
Original Murder Charge Also Stands, San Francisco District Attorney Announces
No Speedy Release in Bail for Film Star, Despite Grand Jury Action

(San Francisco, Sept. 14.) Two charges today had been placed against Roscoe "Fatty" Arbuckle, motion picture star, in connection with the death of Miss Virginia Rappe, film actress. The San Francisco County grand jury late last night voted an indictment charging manslaughter, but District Attorney Matthew Brady declared the prosecution on a murder complaint already underway in the justice court would not be halted.

The grand jury indictment does not come within the province of the justice court, but goes direct to the Superior Court, where it is returnable next Thursday. A warrant for the film comedian's arrest on the manslaughter charge is expected to be issued Friday, the District Attorney said.

The murder complaint was sworn to Monday by Mrs. Bambina Delmont, a close friend of Miss Rappe.

The grand jury indictment came after two sessions, each lasting many hours. At last night's session Zey

Prevost and Alice Blake, showgirls, testified, and Grace Holsten, a nurse, who attended Miss Rappe, was closeted with the jury.

Zey Prevost and Alice Blake were guests at the party where Miss Rappe is alleged to have suffered injuries from which she died.

The grand jury's voting of indictment charging a lesser offense than murder will not make Arbuckle eligible for bail at once, the District Attorney declared:

"He will not be able to obtain temporary liberty on bail until the charge of murder is disposed of," Brady said. "If the murder charge is withdrawn, he will be able to obtain his freedom, pending hearing on the manslaughter charge."

Zey Prevost, before the grand jury, is said to have altered statements she made to District Attorney Brady last Sunday, which brought charges from Brady that the witnesses had been intimidated. Alice Blake in her testimony corroborated Miss Prevost's statements, it was said.

Miss Halston told of being present at the postmortem on the body of Miss Rappe, which was performed by Dr. William Ophuls and Dr. M. E. Rumwell last week.

Among witnesses before the grand jury, some of whom later testified at the second day's proceedings of the coroner's inquest, were Mrs. Bambina Maude Delmont, Al Semnacher, Miss Rappe's manager, Miss Prevost and Miss Blake, all of whom are said to have been present at the Arbuckle party, and Mrs. Jean Jameson, a nurse who attended Miss Rappe before her death.

One of the chief developments of the afternoon was the reappearance of Alice Blake, missing witness.

She was brought to the Hall of Justice by Frank Jones, who declared that he was an old-time friend and had located her as soon as he learned she was missing.

According to Jones, she disappeared to save her wealthy family from publicity. He said her real name was Alice Westphal and that she was a daughter of a wealthy Oakland capitalist.

Mrs. Delmont at the inquest yesterday said she, Miss Rappe and Al Semnacher drove to San Francisco from Los Angeles, arriving Sunday night September 4.

While she and Miss Rappe were eating breakfast the next day, a telephone call was received; Mr. Arbuckle wanted to see them all at the St. Francis Hotel. Miss Rappe went to Arbuckle's room alone, she said, and then telephoned to Mrs. Delmont and Semnacher to join her.

There, she testified, she met Arbuckle, Lowell Sherman, Ira G. Fortlouis and Frederick Fishback. There were many bottles on the table in the room. Miss Rappe had three drinks of gin and orange juice and Mrs. Delmont had about ten drinks of whiskey. Two more girls came in, whom she learned later were Alice Blake and Zey Prevost.

Miss Rappe rose, she said, and went into the bathroom off Arbuckle's room. When she came out of the bathroom Arbuckle was in his room. He closed the door between it and the sitting room where the other members of the party were.

She heard screams coming from the room about an hour later, she said, and demanded that Arbuckle open the door. He did so. Miss Rappe was on the bed staring at her clothes and screaming:

"I am hurt. I am dying. He did it."

She removed the girl's clothing and, assisted by Fishback, placed her in a tub of cold water. This had no effect. So Miss Rappe was taken to another room and put to bed.

Arbuckle kept his eyes fixed on the witness throughout her testimony.

Mrs. Delmont finished her testimony at noon. Arbuckle took more than usual interest when, toward the close of the session, corner Dr. T. B. W. Leland asked the witness:

"How do you happen to remember what happened if you had so many drinks of whiskey?"

"My memory is always good," she answered.

When the inquest was resumed in the afternoon Ira G. Fortlouis, a salesman, took the stand. He testified that he was present at the party, but left before Arbuckle is supposed to have gone into a bedroom with Miss Rappe.

Mr. Semnacher testified that he attended the party after trying in vain to induce Miss Rappe to return to Los Angeles. He was not present, he said during the alleged attack, but came back later and saw Miss Rappe on the bed apparently very ill.

Semnacher also testified that he visited Miss Rappe the day following the party and she said to him:

"Roscoe hurt me."

He said he did not hear the screaming testified to by Mrs. Delmont and was surprised when he heard the full details of the party from Mrs. Delmont the next day.

Before the grand jury, Mrs. Delmont also testified regarding the occurrences at the party. <u>She had repeatedly knocked and kicked at the closed door behind which were Arbuckle and Miss Rappe, she said, and finally compelled Arbuckle to open it</u>. She told of having attended the stricken girl and of the girl's removal to the Wakefield Sanitarium from the hotel.

Mrs. Jean Jameson, one of the nurses who had attended to Miss Rappe at the sanitarium, testified that <u>Miss Rappe had told her that Arbuckle had treated her</u>

roughly and that Arbuckle had said that he had waited five years for the girl. At times Miss Rappe said she did not remember what happened in the room and at other times, she accused Arbuckle of hurting her, Mrs. Jameson testified. Dr. William Ophuls, who performed the postmortem on Miss Rappe, and Ira G. Fortlouis and Al Semnacher, guests of the party, also testified.

Fatty's Wife Goes to Him As "Friend"

(New York, Sept. 14.) Mrs. Roscoe Arbuckle, who was known professionally as Minta Durfee, left New York today for San Francisco to help her husband, if possible, although she has been separated from him for five years.

"I am going to him because I think it is my duty to be near him," she said. "I want to help him in every way I can. I don't know just how I can be of service to him, but many things will turn up that I can do.

"When we were married I was 17 and my husband was 21. That was back in 1908. Five years ago, we agreed to disagree, and I receive a separate maintenance. Unfortunately – or perhaps fortunately, as you please – there are no children. We were not bitter against each other. We simply decided that we would remain good friends. Mr. Arbuckle has been very generous in his treatment of me in regard to finances. I have not had to work during these years, and last February he made me a present of a fine automobile.

"A reconciliation? That depends upon whether I find that my place is with him and whether he is ready for a return to the life we led when we were married, when I was his inspiration. All I know now is that I'm going to a friend who needs every bit of help he can get."

Mrs. Arbuckle was accompanied on the trip to San Francisco by her mother, Mrs. Flora Durfee, of Los Angeles.

[*Evening Public Ledger*, September 14, 1921]
Says "Fatty" Used Stardom As a Lure.
Miss Rappe's Friend Declares Arbuckle Held the Promise of Better Job
Wanted To Talk Business

(San Francisco, Sept. 14.) The lure of "something better" in her motion picture career, possibly the stardom she had craved for years but never had attained, was the snare with which Roscoe Arbuckle, charged with her murder, enticed Virginia Rappe into his net.

This is one of the charges Mrs. Bambina Maude Delmont has made in her complaint against Arbuckle. The police have not yet seen fit to make public her entire story, and this feature of her disclosure is one of the important circumstances the authorities have kept to themselves.

Though for five years a member of the Hollywood colony and during that period intimately acquainted with all the fascinations of the motion picture "game," Miss Rappe proved to be just as susceptible to the lure of motion picture advancement as are hundreds of thousands of girls who have never achieved the screen and will forever dream of accomplishing it.

Miss Rappe's death from injuries alleged to have been inflicted by Arbuckle in the sensational party in his St. Francis Hotel suite is directly due, avers Mrs. Delmont, to happy hope that <u>through her participation in the party she would obtain higher position in her field</u>.

Mrs. Delmont was hostess to Miss Rappe at the Delmont home, in Fresno, Saturday. The two motored into San Francisco Sunday and put up at the Palace Hotel. There, as they were strolling through the lobby Sunday afternoon, she has told the police in a statement which the authorities have not entirely disclosed, they saw Arbuckle and another man.

The other man was Ira Fortlouis. Mrs. Delmont said she has learned that Fortlouis, a salesman for a New York garment house, turned to Arbuckle and with a tone of rapt admiration, explained:

"Gee, but she is a peach! I'd like to meet her."

Arbuckle, with a <u>dramatic gesture of possession</u>, replied proudly:

"Well, I can fix that up. She's a friend of mine. Leave it to me."

The next day, in their suite at the Palace Hotel, Mrs. Delmont received a telephone call. It was from Arbuckle. He asked for Miss Rappe.

The latter at first hesitated, expressing her repulsion against Arbuckle. Finally, however, she went to the telephone. Her talk with Arbuckle was interrupted several times as Miss Rappe, with her hand over the mouthpiece, turned to her companion and reported what Arbuckle was saying. She said:

"<u>He wants me to go to his room at the St. Francis</u>."

Mrs. Delmont replied:

"Be careful of him. What does he want?"

"<u>He says he's got a chance to get me something better in the movies</u> and maybe it's a chance to make a star out of me."

Pondering for a moment, Mrs. Delmont warned:

"I don't trust him. You know his reputation. You think it's safe for you to go?"

Miss Rappe answered:

"He says he's giving a party and wants me to go to talk this thing over with him. I don't want to lose the chance, but I'm afraid. I don't like that man and I'm afraid of him."

Mrs. Delmont cautioned:

"Tell him you'll come if I can accompany you."

Turning to the telephone, the actress asked whether Arbuckle would invite Mrs. Delmont to his party. He replied affirmatively and she accepted the invitation.

The two women went to the St. Francis suite. There they found the party already in full swing, with an abundance of liquor on the tables and men and women singing and pranking with hilarity <u>attesting the enthusiasm with which the intoxicants had been attacked</u>.

Arbuckle, himself already strongly influenced by drinks, laughed off Miss Rappe's suggestion that they get right down to business of the moving picture proposition he had spoken of. He gayly pushed that topic into the future saying he would take it up with Miss Rappe later during the party.

Nevertheless, he continued to play his lure strongly. In vague manner he brought up time and again the fact that he had for Miss Rappe an opportunity that she could not afford to ignore, but he never came down to "brass tacks" as to what the job was.

It is understood, from what Mrs. Delmont says, that <u>Arbuckle made a "proposition" that Miss Rappe resented</u>.

In the course of this dispute, during which Arbuckle's zest for Miss Rappe had caused him to discard his earlier purpose of giving her company to his New York friend, Arbuckle, it is alleged, dragged the actress into his room "to talk it over privately."

[*The New York Herald*, September 14, 1921]
Testimony at inquest

A dramatic recital of events at the party was given at the resumption of the coroner's inquest this morning. Mrs. Delmont was the witness. Under examination by Coroner Leland, she went over in detail the entire story as previously told of the drinking and dancing and in regard to the episode which led, it is said, to Virginia Rappe's death

"Miss Rappe went into the bathroom alone," she said. "Arbuckle took hold of her, she told me afterward. I was not paying much attention to them. There was not much familiarity on the part of the men up to this time. I was warm with dancing and borrowed a pair of Sherman's pajamas and put them on in his room. When I came back, they told me Virginia was in a room with Arbuckle. I was angry and, taking off my shoe, rapped on the door with the heel. They were in there an hour and I heard her screaming. I telephoned to the manager and, while doing so, Arbuckle came out. He had Miss Rappe's Panama hat on his head. Miss Rappe cried out when we went in to her, 'I am hurt! I'm dying! He did it!'"

Asked by a juror if Miss Rappe made any objection when Arbuckle went into the room with her, the witness answered, "No."

At police headquarters, it was reported today that the complete list of visitors to Arbuckle's rooms included more than thirty names. Statements comparing the party with similar events in Los Angeles have been received.

The testimony of Al Semnacher at the inquest did not strengthen Brady's evidence. Semnacher declared he had not seen Mrs. Delmont knock on the door. This may have been due to the fact that he did not remain in Arbuckle's room during the entire visit of Mrs. Delmont and Miss Rappe, but made a short visit to friends in the neighborhood, it was explained.

The testimony of Vera Cumberland and Jean Jameson, two nurses in attendance on Miss Rappe, threw new light on the case. According to Mrs. Jameson, Miss Rappe took her into her confidence concerning her romance with Henry Lehrman, the motion picture director who now is in New York. <u>Miss Cumberland's testimony was sensational</u> and was the first evidence made public which explained the confidence expressed by the prosecutor in his ability to bring the case within the limitations of murder as defined by the California statutes.

Under the law<u>, it must be shown that the commission of a criminal act, or an attempt, led into the death of the victim</u>.

Miss Rappe's statement, as repeated under oath by Miss Cumberland, was the first indication that the prosecutor intends to try to prove the charge by direct as well as circumstantial evidence.

With the day's developments, the authorities believe they have rounded up all the essential witnesses with the exception of two women who were at the party. These were May Parsons and Mrs. May Taube. Mrs. Taube, it was stated, was located at Sacramento and May Parsons is still being sought. What the state expects to prove by these women was not intimated by Brady nor did he disclose whether he would be embarrassed by failure to discover Miss Parsons.

It was hinted that the failure of the grand jury to indict at Monday night's session was due to the conflict of testimony between Mrs. Delmont and one or two of those called last night. Calling them for the special session was taken as an indication that Brady expected them to correct their testimony on some points.

Sensations at inquest

Sensation followed sensation during the second day of the inquest. Beginning in the morning, when Mrs. Delmont, companion of the girl, testified at great length, through a long afternoon.

When other members of Arbuckle's party and nurses told their stories, <u>the crowd that packed the hearing room at the morgue received full measure of that for which they had come.</u>

Jean Jameson, one of the nurses, was called upon to testify concerning an examination she made of her patient in the Wakefield Sanitarium. As a result of this she said Miss Rappe told of her relations with her sweetheart, Henry Lehrman. Jameson's testimony concerning Miss Rappe's statements to her caused a stir in the audience.

Later Miss Vera Cumberland, another nurse in the case, testified that Miss Rapp was exceedingly anxious that word of the party be kept from Lehrman's ears, as she said they had had a disagreement and her sweetheart might "say it was spite work."

Again, <u>Miss Cumberland caused a sensation when, very reluctantly, she declared her conscience forced her to withdraw from all connection with the treatment of Miss Rappe</u> on September 8.

"My conscience didn't permit me to handle the case further," she said in response to Coroner Leland's questions, "because in my opinion it had been handled negligently. I had no trouble with Dr. M. E. Rumwell, but we did have a conversation on the matter."

Through the testimony of Mrs. Delmont and Al Semnacher, both of whom accompanied Virginia Rappe on the automobile trip north which started from Los Angeles early in the morning of September 3, details of the formation of the party were revealed.

Semnacher "financed" the expedition to San Francisco. His friendship with Mrs. Delmont was of some years standing. They met in front of a Los Angeles candy store a few days prior to September 3, and Mrs. Delmont expressed the wish that someone would take her to Fresno on a business trip.

"I asked Miss Rappe if she cared to accompany us," Semnacher testified, "and she said she was very glad to go. And when we got to Selma, Miss Rappe said, 'let's go on to San Francisco, having come this far.'"

Both Mrs. Delmont and Semnacher gave testimony very similar to their published versions of the affair, but their accounts are at variance on certain points. The former was emphatic in saying Arbuckle was alone with Miss Rappe in room 1219 at the Hotel St. Francis. She testified that she heard Miss Rappe scream, which led her to telephone to the hotel office.

"Mr. Arbuckle heard the call up on the telephone," Mrs. Delmont continued. "And he opened the door and said: 'She's in here.' He was in his pajamas and had her Panama hat on his head."

Mrs. Delmont was frank to admit she partook freely of the liquor provided at the Arbuckle party. Before leaving Los Angeles, she said she "had a few drinks," and she took a pint of whiskey for the trip north. At Selma, she had six drinks. But she was emphatic in saying that neither Miss Rappe nor Semnacher touched a drink until they arrived at the St. Francis. There, Mrs. Delmont said, Miss Rappe "had three drinks in about the first hour."

"It impressed me that Mr. Arbuckle was more intoxicated than anyone else in the party," she testified. "He was just a little gone. He showed it in his eyes and being very talkative. He was not staggering or anything of that sort."

She said that after she had changed from her walking suit into a suit of pajamas, having become warm from dancing, she was conscious that Virginia was absent from the main party.

"I asked the others where Virginia was," she said. "I called to her and didn't get any answer. I took the shoes I had on with French heels and kicked at the door to room 1219. I kicked with all my might. There was no answer. I didn't hear a sound. Then I telephoned to the desk clerk."

Al Semnacher, when called to the witness stand, told Coroner Leland he would stand by his statement as given to the police. He declared he left the Arbuckle party twice to make visits around the city.

"I don't drink at all," he said, "and I was more anxious to get back to Los Angeles than to stay with the party.

"When I returned, Miss Rappe was not in room 1220, the reception room, but Arbuckle was there. I was surprised the next morning when Mrs. Delmont told me of the screams. I hadn't heard them.

"I heard Miss Rappe say Tuesday morning when Mrs. Delmont sent for me, 'Roscoe hurt me.' That was all she said, and it was her first reference to Mr. Arbuckle. Previously on several occasions she had made the remark, 'I am dying,' at the same time placing her hands on her abdomen.

"Until that Tuesday morning, I had no idea she had been hurt. We all thought she was intoxicated."

Miss Rappe, Semnacher said, very seldom touched liquor, and "I have seen her take one or two drinks and get dizzy."

He was called on to identify garments worn by Miss Rappe when she went to the hotel which have been recovered by the police here and in Los Angeles. When the girl's Panama hat was shown to him Semnacher said he had never seen Arbuckle wearing it.

Ira G. Fortlouis, a New York salesman who was a member of the Arbuckle party, gave his version of the affair. He could not recall seeing anyone intoxicated nor did he see either Arbuckle or Miss Rappe leaving the room. It was not until the following day that he heard there had been trouble, he said.

Mrs. Jameson testified that Miss Rappe made conflicting statements to her.

[*Bisbee Daily Review*, September 17 1921]
Forty Quarts of Liquor Consumed at Fatty's Party
Federal Officials Continue Probe to Learn Source of Liquor

(Los Angeles, Sept 16.) A federal investigation here into the source of the liquor reported to have been in evidence at the Roscoe ("Fatty") Arbuckle party in a San Francisco hotel following which the death of Miss Virginia Rappe occurred, was continued here today under United States District Attorney Robert O'Connor and E. Forrest Mitchell, Federal Prohibition Director for California.

It was announced by federal officers that every individual in attendance at the party who can be located here will be examined and that later the federal grand jury will be summoned to hear the result of the investigation.

Lowell Sherman, actor, told the federal officers that liquor was furnished to the party by the chef of the hotel, who he said was known as "Tony."

Subpoenas were issued today for summoning Lowell Sherman and [*Fred*] Fishback, declared to have been guests at the Labor Day party in the rooms of Roscoe C. ("Fatty") Arbuckle.

Sherman and Fishback were questioned yesterday concerning liquor alleged to have been consumed at the Arbuckle party.

According to Robert Camarillo, assistant United States District Attorney, Fishback said more than forty quarts of liquor were consumed in three days at the Arbuckle apartments.

Will Face Court on Murder Charge at Early Date
District Attorney and Police Decide To Prosecute On Most Serious Charge
Physician Is Sought
Doctor Who First Attended Miss Rappe Missing

(San Francisco, Sept. 16.) The way was clear today for the trial of Roscoe C. ("Fatty") Arbuckle, motion picture comedian, on a charge of murder resulting from the death of Miss Virginia Rappe, motion picture actress in a sanitarium here Friday, September 9, after she is alleged to have been attacked at a party given by Arbuckle at his rooms in the St. Francis Hotel Monday, September 6.

The returning of four charges against Arbuckle, two for murder and two for manslaughter, necessitated conferences during the week between District Attorney Brady and police officials as to the exact charge on which he shall be tried.

It was decided today that charge should be murder and the police court in which Arbuckle's case is pending was so advised.

The undertaking establishment having the body of Miss Rappe announced that it would be sent to Los Angeles tonight for interment in the Hollywood Cemetery.

Physician sought

A new development today was the announcement that Dr. Arthur Beardslee, house physician at the St. Francis, who was the physician who first attended Miss Rappe, is being sought by the authorities. Milton T. U'Ren, Assistant District Attorney announced late today that the police detectives had been unable to locate him and asked the newspapers to assist in the search.

Dr. Beardslee is wanted for the purpose of giving testimony before the grand jury regarding certain phases of the medical attention given Miss Rappe, U'Ren said.

Bigger crowds than usual greeted Arbuckle's public appearance today. A few moments before his case was called in Police Judge Sylvain J. Lazarus' court for a preliminary hearing on one of the murder charges, mostly men attempted to rush through the doors. They were pushed back by police.

Members of the women's vigilante committee, formed for the purpose of assisting the police and prosecuting officials of the city in maintaining law and order, were present at the court hearing.

Following the court session, District Attorney Brady gave a statement in which he explained the reason for his determination to press the murder charge. Later in the day, he appeared before the finance committee of the county board of supervisors and asked that a special fund be provided for him with which to prosecute the Arbuckle case.

Arbuckle must appear in the court of Superior Judge Harold Louderback tomorrow to be arraigned on one of the two manslaughter charges against him. The charge is that voted by the grand jury Wednesday. The arraignment is merely a formal proceeding, however, but Arbuckle, if he desires, may plead on the charge or the District Attorney may make a motion to have it held in abeyance until the murder charge is disposed of.

Arbuckle's next appearance on the murder charge has been set for next Thursday at 1:00 PM in Judge Lazarus' court, at which time it is expected that he will be given his preliminary examination.

Mrs. Delmont collapses

Mrs. Bambina Maude Delmont, who swore to the murder charge against Arbuckle on which he appeared in court today, viewed Miss Rappe's body today and is reported to have suffered a partial collapse after leaving the undertaking establishment. The manager of the establishment said that the body, according to present plans, will be taken to Los Angeles on the Lark, a Southern Pacific Company express train, tonight.

Robert H. McCormack, Assistant United States Attorney General in charge of liquor prohibition prosecutions, said that he expected to present to the federal grand jury Tuesday evidence that liquor was served and consumed at the St. Francis Hotel party given by Arbuckle, in which Miss Rappe was alleged to have received her fatal injuries.

Vote funds for Arbuckle trial

(San Francisco, Sept. 16.) The finance committee of the Board of Supervisors told District Attorney Matt Brady that he might have $1,000 at once in addition to his regular budget allowance for the prosecution of Roscoe ("Fatty") Arbuckle and that more money would be supplied him as he needed it.

"We will see other great expense," Brady explained. "The defendant is reputed to be wealthy, and there will be a great deal of money spent defending him. If we do not get sufficient funds we may meet with disaster."

[*The Seattle Star*, September 17, 1921]
Murder!
In First-Degree
Why Charge Brought In Arbuckle Case

Why was "Fatty" Arbuckle charged with first-degree murder?

Why was the manslaughter charge dropped?

Or, why was he not charged with criminal assault, or rape?

The answer lies in information in the hands of District Attorney Matt Brady, information not yet public.

Arbuckle will face trial under a special section of the criminal code. <u>It is section 189</u>. Under this section, murder to be first-degree need not be perpetrated as the result of malice.

A man may commit first-degree murder while engaged in or attempting to engage in the perpetration of another felony – such as arson, rape, robbery, burglary or mayhem.

All murder which is perpetrated by means of poison, or lying in wait, torture, or any other means of willful, deliberate and premeditated killing, OR WHICH IS COMMITTED IN THE PERPETRATION OR ATTEMPT TO PERPETRATE arson, RAPE, murder, burglary, or mayhem, is MURDER OF THE FIRST-DEGREE! And all other kinds of murder are the second-degree.

<u>Had Miss Rappe's death been caused by accident, Arbuckle could only have been charged with manslaughter</u>. From the fact that District Attorney Brady, after a thorough investigation, had Arbuckle charged with first-

degree murder, it being taken in legal circles to show that he has information that <u>Arbuckle either perpetrated or attempted to perpetrate criminal assault upon the girl</u>, the act or acts of which resulted in her death.

Dr. William Ophuls, who made a postmortem examination of the dead girl's body, gave out a statement that "<u>there was absolutely no evidence of criminal assault</u>, no signs that the girl had been attacked in any way."

District Attorney Brady evidently has information to the effect that either the girl was assaulted or that she was killed in an attempted assault.

First-degree murder carries two alternatives – death by hanging or life imprisonment, the jury to determine which.

With no malice motive, it may be difficult to find the jury that would fix the maximum penalty. Should a plea of guilty be entered, the penalty is fixed by the judge.

[*Washington Times*, September 17, 1921]

Clown Is Afraid Of Crowd at Hearings
"Stay Close To Me," Arbuckle Pleads To Guards
St. Francis Doctor Sought

(San Francisco, Sept 17.) A determined search is underway today for Dr. Arthur Beardslee, house physician of the St. Francis Hotel and first to attend Virginia Rappe, for whose alleged murder Roscoe "Fatty" Arbuckle, famous clown of the screen, must stand trial.

So far as is known, Dr. Beardslee has never made a statement.

A chance remark by the defense in the course of a heated argument over delay of the preliminary hearing caused District Attorney Brady's office to institute a statewide search for the doctor.

"There was a certain medical testimony which we are at present unfamiliar," Frank Dominguez, chief counsel for Arbuckle, said.

Immediately, the search of the state for Dr. Beardslee was underway. The prosecution is desirous of getting his full testimony and of learning if the defense already had an inkling of what he will say. The physician, so far as can be learned, saw Miss Rappe and left the next day on a long hunting trip.

What his diagnosis was and what medical treatment he accorded the patient are points that both the state and defense are anxious to have answered.

Rivaling this report in interest was the report current locally that Henry Lehrman, fiancée of Miss Rappe, was engaging William Travers Jerome, New York attorney, as a special prosecutor. The District Attorney had no confirmation of such a move and was inclined to regard it as unnecessary.

Arraignment today

Arbuckle was scheduled for another courtroom appearance today.

He must appear before Judge Harold Louderback in Superior Court for arraignment on a continuance of the manslaughter charge which will be held in abeyance. It is unlikely that it will ever be used, inasmuch as the jury which hears the evidence against Arbuckle on the murder charge will have power to fix a lesser degree, including manslaughter, if in their belief he is guilty of a crime, but in a lesser degree than charged by the state.

There were prospects of another big crowd at today's arraignment and precautions were taken early to prevent yesterday's scenes when more than 100 men of a huge crowd filling the courtroom corridor broke the door of

Judge Lazarus' court room and had to be forcibly ejected. One man was trampled but not seriously injured.

Arbuckle fears the crowds. As he descended the elevator from the city prison to the courtroom level yesterday and saw the crowd surging about, he was heard to remark to his two guards:

"Stay close to me."

His chief of counsel, Frank Dominguez, went to Los Angeles last night. A reservation had been made for Arbuckle, but it was canceled when all hopes for bail faded after District Attorney Brady announced his intention of proceeding with the murder charge.

Milton Cohen and Charles Brennan are looking after the prisoner's interests until the return of Dominguez.

Medical testimony

There is increasing indication that medical testimony is to play a great part in the trial. It is to assume a prominent part in the preliminary hearing and at the trial resolve itself into a battle of the best medical experts obtainable by each side.

There was a report today that counsel for Arbuckle even hopes to secure Arbuckle's absolute freedom at the preliminary hearing through startling medical testimony in which they place reliance. It is understood it was this report that sent the state scurrying in an effort to find Dr. Beardslee.

When District Attorney Matthew Brady, in the court of Police Judge Sylvian Lazarus yesterday, announced that "the people are ready to proceed on the murder charge," he blasted hopes of the defense that Arbuckle would be given his liberty on $5,000 bond, which was set by the court when a grand jury indictment charging the defendant with manslaughter was returned.

It was indicated that the prosecution's decision to go on trial on the murder charge was a surprise to the defense.

From Los Angeles came reports that Arbuckle already had made train reservations for a trip from San Francisco to that city last evening. Murder is not a bailable charge in California.

Women Guarded Until "Fatty" Goes On Trial
Witnesses Kept in Strict Seclusion under D.A.'s Orders

(San Francisco, Calif., Sept. 17.) Women witnesses scheduled to take the stand for the prosecution in the case of the people versus Roscoe "Fatty" Arbuckle have suddenly disappeared from the public eye.

While a curious city impatiently awaits their testimony at the trial, they spend the hours in deepest meditation and solitude.

The foresight of the District Attorney has placed them in the very heart of seclusion, each within a private home. They are under heavy constant guard.

"The women are under voluntary seclusion," District Attorney Matthew Brady explained today when questioned on the whereabouts of the prospective witnesses.

Removed from the maddening presence of those who with her passed through the tragic party scene following which Virginia Rappe died, Mrs. Bambina Maude Delmont is slowly acquiring the strength to help her through the coming ordeal of judge and jury.

Less tragic are the hours in their procession for pretty and dainty Alice Blake, whose eyes have also seen and who, too, has heard and knows the details of the Arbuckle party in the St. Francis. Alice appears to be reaping full benefit of her "vacation," as she calls it.

And somewhere in San Francisco is Zey Prevost. Nor are her thoughts on those who wait and watch upon her. She, too, will tell what she knows about the "lil' party" and her share in it when requested to take the stand.

Other women who will be called are Miss Vera Cumberland, whose testimony during the inquest startled the courtroom, and Mrs. Jean Jameson, another nurse, the first to attend the deceased through the agonizing hours that preceded death.

When the case is called, then will these women step out from obscurity and tell of the indelible scenes that have burned and seared themselves into their conscience.

[*Washington Times*, September 20, 1921]

Arbuckle Chum and Witness Is In Chicago
Prosecutor Investigates Plot to Discredit Testimony of Girl at Fatal Party

(Chicago, Sept. 20.) Lowell Sherman, actor, sought by authorities of San Francisco as a witness in the case of Roscoe ("Fatty") Arbuckle, charged with the murder of Virginia Rappe, arrived in Chicago today.

He entered a denial to reports that he was a fugitive from justice and that a second man was in the room where Miss Rappe met death.

"No one but Arbuckle knows what happened to Virginia in that inner room," Sherman said. "That's all talk about another man being in that chamber.

"I'm not a fugitive from justice. I was allowed to come east after giving voluminous depositions.

"Another point I want to make clear is that Arbuckle, who is my friend, never carried Miss Rappe into his boudoir while he was clothed only in his pajamas. That's tommyrot."

(San Francisco, Sept. 20.) When the County grand jury adjourned early today after a five-hour session, District Attorney Brady announced important progress had been made towards establishing that a "frame up" had existed to impeach the testimony of Miss Zey Prevost, one of the state's star witnesses in the case of Roscoe "Fatty" Arbuckle, charged with the murder of Virginia Rappe, film actress.

Missing witness found.

District Attorney Brady received word today that Mrs. May Parsons, a minor witness in the case, who disappeared shortly after the initial investigation, has been located by detectives in Texas. He has not decided whether or not her return will be sought.

Lowell Sherman, actor friend of Arbuckle, and companion at the hotel party, has not been located.

Dr. Arthur Beardslee, who was to have testified before the grand jury last night, failed to arrive. District Attorney Brady will question him upon his return from his hunting trip, which has prevented his evidence being available until now. But State and defense are anxious to learn Dr. Beardslee's diagnosis of Miss Rappe's case and the nature of the medical treatment given.

Tampering with witnesses

Discussing the grand jury investigation, Brady made the following statement today:

"[Reginald] Morely was forced to admit before the grand jury that he and [Joyce] Clark had discussed the subject of making money through her acting as a witness for the defense.

"It also developed that before coming to the jury, Morely and [Dr. Gabor] Kingstone had visited Milton Cohen, one of Arbuckle's attorneys, and asked him what they should testify before the grand jury. They said he told them to tell the whole truth.

"After questioning, the Clark woman admitted the subject of making money in the Arbuckle case was discussed several times before Morely, Kingstone and Mrs. Morely.

"She said Morely wanted her to impeach the testimony of Zey Prevost, a prosecution witness.

"Neither Morely nor Kingstone had ever discussed the case with the Prevost woman, they told the grand jury.

"Morely, however, according to the Clark woman, had suggested to her that she see Miss Prevost and Miss Alice Blake, another of our witnesses, and tell them to leave town."

Search for a new woman witness

Edna C. Grant, a nurse who attended Virginia Rappe, today became an outstanding development in the case.

Information that the prosecution and defense alike attached the greatest degree of importance to information Miss Grant is believed to hold in regard to the medical treatment of the girl, came as no small surprise in view of previously reiterated statements that all important witnesses have been found.

Miss Grant, it is known, attended Virginia Rappe for a time at the outset, then quit the case abruptly.

The authorities want to know why. So does the defense.

<u>The rumor has been persistent of late that Virginia Rappe's death was due, not to Arbuckle's actions directly, but to a fault in the medical treatment of the case.</u>

Miss Grant talked freely to friends before she went "into the silence."

"Too much high life"

Dr. Beardslee, when found in Bridgeport on his hunting trip, told the County Sheriff:

"I know little of the case. The girl appeared to be suffering from too much high life. I found no trace of injury in treating her."

<u>The entire trial may hinge on the point whether Miss Rappe's internal rupture was caused by the Arbuckle incidents, by natural causes complicated by disease and intoxication, or by medical error.</u>

Arbuckle and his wife, Mrs. Minta Durfee Arbuckle, having forgotten their five years' separation, were happy today following a reconciliation within the bleak gray walls of the prison guestroom.

There were no hysterics at this "party." There were no tears.

The actor kissed his wife and felt her lips returning his caress. For the first brief moments, she clung to and embraced her husband tenderly. His wife's is the first feminine presence and sympathy the comedian has known since the night of the party at the St. Francis Hotel.

Happy at reconciliation

Arbuckle looked happily and lovingly at his wife.

To her he poured out all the burning confidence of his heart. To her he smiled for the first time since his imprisonment, and for her he looked with all the gratitude of a grateful slave.

Minta Durfee Arbuckle is diminutive. She has very large blue eyes and henna-hued hair. Clad in a modish suit of tan and furred and hatted in the best of taste and style, she held to the portly arm of her husband, pledging loyalty and love.

The prison clock seriously timed their minutes together into two hours and a half. Unaware of the big cardboard placard that proclaims but "20 minutes a day allowed visitors," Arbuckle and his wife sat and dreamily planned into the future.

Darkness settled over the prison room when the Arbuckles parted.

"Goodbye, my husband," Mrs. Arbuckle whispered and looked into her husband's eyes and smiled.

After a conference with Arbuckle's attorneys, Mrs. Arbuckle yesterday issued the following statement:

"Upon my arrival in San Francisco to aid in the defense of my husband, I have only one request to make to the fair-minded people of this city. I simply asked them to be fair to Mr. Arbuckle, to give him only that to which he is entitled and for which San Francisco is noted around the world – a square deal.

"I know, and all his friends know, that he is innocent. He is entitled to a trial by a jury made up of men and women whose minds will be receptive alone to the truth. Only one side of the story has been told, and I know the people of this good city will be willing to wait until the other side comes out in proper, orderly fashion in court.

"I believe all will agree with me that first impressions gained from rumors and reports are most of the times, upon close investigation, found to be false. I know when the truth is heard in this matter – when the entire story has been unfolded – that my husband will be completely exonerated, that his good name will be thoroughly cleared, and that he will again take his former place in the hearts of the American people.

"In asking the people to suspend judgment now, I am asking no more than any wife or mother would ask, placed in the same position I occupy."

After the issuance of the statement, Mrs. Arbuckle and her mother were whisked away to quarters already arranged for them. The attorneys intimated that they would be secluded for the present at least.

[*The Washington Times*, September 22, 1921]

"Fatty" Confessed Attack on Virginia, Says Manager
Friend Says Fatty Admitted Treating Miss Rappe with Ice

(Los Angeles, Sept. 22.) Roscoe ("Fatty") Arbuckle applied a piece of ice to Miss Virginia Rappe's body when he was alone with her in a bedroom of his suite at the hotel St. Francis, San Francisco, on the day of his now notorious party there, according to statements made before the Los Angeles County grand jury by Al Semnacher, the dead film girl's former manager.

According to Acting District Attorney William C. Doran, the application of this ice "possibly could have brought on the condition found by the autopsy surgeon who made the postmortem examination of the girl's body in San Francisco. The condition was a rupture of the bladder, and this rupture was said to have been the likely cause of peritonitis, from which they found she died."

Doran continued with the explanation that nothing in the statement of Semnacher itself could be understood as meaning that Arbuckle had applied the ice forcibly, but Doran added that "if the ice was forcibly applied, and if other circumstances were unfavorable to the girl, the serious condition referred to could have been brought about."

While pointing out that the matter of force was one at present of deduction, the District Attorney's office at the same time hailed Semnacher's testimony as perhaps the most important the state so far has secured against Arbuckle.

Semnacher's story was that Arbuckle had told him, in the presence of Fred Fishback, Lowell Sherman, and Harry McCullough, Arbuckle's chauffeur, that he had used the ice on Miss Rappe during the time he was alone in his bedroom with the girl, while the drinking party was going on in the sitting room.

Arbuckle made this confession, Semnacher said, the day after the incident, and at that time, Semnacher told the inquisitorial body, his party had not learned that Miss Rappe's condition had become critical.

[September 23, 1921]
Probe Tells of Night in Arbuckle's Rooms
Witnesses at Police Court
Result of Examination Will Determine Whether Film Comedian Is To Be Bound Over to Superior Court

(San Francisco, Sept. 22.) The Police Court examination of Roscoe ("Fatty") Arbuckle, which will determine whether the film comedian is to be bound over to the Superior Court for trial on a charge of the murder of Miss Virginia Rappe, began here today in a courtroom filled almost exclusively with women[5].

Three witnesses who saw Miss Rappe's body after her death September 9, which, it is charged, resulted from injuries suffered at a drinking party four days before in Arbuckle's hotel suite, testified that they observed bruises on her limbs and body. Two of them, the surgeon who performed the postmortem examination and the autopsy

---

[5] Women had only recently won the right to vote and were not shy in demonstrating their influence in law and policy.

surgeon, said the <u>death was from a ruptured bladder, caused, in their opinion, by external force</u>.

The autopsy surgeon also told of a small puncture he said he found in the left arm of the body, which he attributed to a hypodermic needle.

At tomorrow's session it is expected there will be introduced testimony regarding incidents at the party, where, according to witnesses at the coroner's inquest, Miss Rappe was found moaning and screaming after having been alone in a room with Arbuckle.

Arbuckle listened intently to today's testimony, his face bearing serious expression.

Mrs. Minta Durfee-Arbuckle, his wife from whom he had been separated for five years, but who came here from New York Monday, sat at his side with her mother, Mrs. Flora Durfee.

Dr. Shelby Strange, who performed the autopsy on Miss Rappe, and Dr. William Ophuls, who made the first postmortem examination, where the principal witnesses today.

Dr. Strange said he found bruises on Miss Rappe's right upper arm, apparently caused by finger marks, two bruises on the lower abdomen and others on the thighs and shins, the cause of which he was unable to state. Dr. Ophuls and Miss Grace Halston, a hospital nurse, who was present at the postmortem, both corroborated Dr. Strange's description of the bruises, and coroner's photographs of the body were offered as evidence.

A tear in the bladder wall was described by Dr. Strange, who said the bladder and other organs had been preserved by Dr. Ophuls.

He said he believed that death came from peritonitis resulting from the ruptured bladder and that <u>the rupture was caused by some external force</u>.

Dr. Ophuls said he was called in for postmortem examination by Dr. M. E. Rumwell, the physician who attended Miss Rappe in most of her last illness. He found the abdomen "horribly distended," he said, as a result of rupture and a congestion of blood in several organs of the lower abdomen.

The rupture, he surmised, was caused by over distention of the bladder, resulting probably from some outside cause.

Miss Halston's statement that <u>she believed the bruises on Miss Rappe's arm were made by the grip of another person</u> prompted a debate over its admissibility between Arbuckle's counsel and Milton T. U'Ren, Assistant District Attorney, who conducted the examination.

Judge Lazarus let the testimony go in. The defense did not cross-examine any of the witnesses and Judge Lazarus put the hearing over until 2 PM tomorrow.

Mrs. Bambina Maude Delmont, the complaining witness, Alice Blake and Zey Prevost, will be among the witnesses tomorrow, the District Attorney announced.

Mrs. Delmont accompanied Miss Rappe and Al Seminacher on the trip from Los Angeles to Selma, Fresno and San Francisco, which ended in Miss Rappe's death.

Although many women unable to get into the courtroom submitted to fate and stood patiently on the stairs leading to the courtroom, others refused to be satisfied and called on Chief of Police O'Brien, demanding their rights as "citizens and taxpayers" to be given a seat in the courtroom.

Semnacher, who called the District Attorney by telephone yesterday from Los Angeles to request that expense money be sent to come to San Francisco to testify, arrived today by automobile. He was taken to the

District Attorney's office immediately and detained there during the hearing.

[September 24 1921]

Doctor Says Injury, not Liquor, Killed Miss Rappe
Injuries of Miss Rappe Outweighed Evidence of Alcoholism, Hotel Physician Declares Girl Showed Symptoms of Internal Hurt When Stricken At Arbuckle Party
Member of Fatal Orgy Tells of Drinking and Dancing in Pajamas That Preceded Beauty's Sudden Illness

(San Francisco, Sept. 24.) Miss Virginia Rappe showed symptoms of internal injury immediately after she was stricken, following the party in Roscoe Arbuckle's rooms, and whatever evidence there may have been of alcoholism was overshadowed by her injuries, declared Dr. Arthur Beardslee, house position of the Hotel St. Francis, in a statement made to Assistant District Attorney Milton U'Ren today. Dr. Beardslee treated Miss Rappe in the early stages of her illness.

Dr. Beardslee returned today from a hunting trip on which he started the day after the Arbuckle affair.

After questioning the physician, Mr. U'Ren said that his explanation of his recent absence and his statement of treating Miss Rappe was "entirely satisfactory." And that he was exonerated of all blame for his absence.

Dr. Beardsley said that on the [evening] of September 6, after examining Miss Rappe, he suspected she was injured.

Dr. Beardslee probably will be put on the stand today in Arbuckle's hearing on a murder charge following the completion of the testimony of Al Semnacher, former manager of Miss Rappe.

Semnacher has not proved a good witness for the state, despite the story he told the Los Angeles grand jury. He is Arbuckle's friend, and while testifying yesterday avoided the prisoner's eyes.

Semnacher, examined by Assistant District Attorney Golden, forgot many things. He forgot some of his testimony at the coroner's inquest. He forgot whether he had said the party was drinking. He forgot some of his own statements a few minutes after he had made them.

The roomful of women, white and colored, who had come to be thrilled, when home rather disappointed.

Semnacher first said he had come to San Francisco in his automobile with Miss Rappe and Mrs. Delmont at 1 o'clock on the night of September 4. They stopped at the Palace Hotel.

The following morning at breakfast, Miss Rappe was paged. Semnacher was not allowed to say who called her or what was said. Soon after, he took the two women to the St. Francis and left them.

About 2 o'clock, he called Arbuckle's room and was invited by Fred Fishback to come up. Arbuckle was there, Lowell Sherman, Ira Fortlouis, Miss Rappe, Mrs. Delmont, Miss Zey Prevost, Miss Alice Blake and Mrs. Mae Taube.

When the witness entered the room, he said, Arbuckle was sitting at a table, eating. He was dressed in slippers, pajamas in a bathrobe. Sherman was dressed in the same manner. All the other men and all the women except Mrs. Delmont were in street attire.

"Some were partaking of liquor," said Semnacher, "or orange juice that could have contained gin or anything else."

"There was some talking, laughing, phonograph playing, drinking," he continued. "They drank out of gin, whiskey and White Rock[6] bottles, and out of bottles without labels.

"I believe Miss Blake and Miss Prevost danced together, and I believe Arbuckle and Sherman danced with the ladies."

Semnacher told of seeing Miss Rappe on the bed.

"What was she doing?"

"Moaning, turning from side to side, and keeping her hands on her abdomen. She was undressed."

"Where were her clothes?"

"Scattered on the floor and lying on various articles of furniture. Her hat and cap on chairs; stockings, garters, shoes on the floor."

"What did she say?"

"She said, 'I am dying, I am dying?'"

Semnacher told them how the women had carried Miss Rappe into the bathtub of cold water and later put her back on the bed.

Semnacher gathered up most of the clothing and took it to room 1227, to which Miss Rappe had been taken. He came back to 1219 to see if he had overlooked anything and found in the wastebasket her torn shirtwaist[7], her torn underwear, a torn cuff with her cuff links on it and the jade bracelet.

He threw the torn garments back into the wastebasket, then took them out again.

"Why did you take them out again?"

"I wanted to keep them and josh Miss Rappe about getting intoxicated and tearing them like that."

"What did you do after Miss Rappe had been taken to a room?"

---

[6] A popular brand of mineral water.

[7] Blouse

"Went back to the party. The music and the dancing and drinking went on while the girl lay dying in the room a few doors away."

[*Bisbee Daily Review*, September 25, 1921]

Semnacher Testifies As Witness for Arbuckle
Fatty's Story of Affair Is Told in Court
Miss Rappe's Manager Writes-out Arbuckle's Account; Refuses to Repeat It

(San Francisco, Sept. 24.) Alfred Semnacher declined to repeat aloud from the witness stand today the details of Roscoe (Fatty) Arbuckle's description of his treatment of Miss Virginia Rappe at the revel which led to the girl's death, but instead wrote them out on a paper which he showed to the attorneys and Police Judge Sylvain Lazarus, who was hearing the murder complaint against the film comedian.

He first said that Arbuckle's story of the incidents, told to himself, Lowell Sherman, Fred Semnacher and Arbuckle's chauffeur, Harry McCullough, caused a general laugh. When the details were demanded, he objected to testifying verbally.

No one remonstrated at Arbuckle's tale, according to the witness, who said it was told in Arbuckle's suite at the Hotel St. Francis where the drinking party had taken place the afternoon before. Other conversation about the affair was limited to discussion of the intoxicated condition of some of the participants, Semnacher said. He testified yesterday that he had only coffee to drink.

In answer to questions from Arbuckle's attorneys, Semnacher said he had observed nothing improper in Arbuckle's actions toward Miss Rappe or any of the other women at the party.

When the news of Miss Rappe's death was brought by a newspaper reporter to Arbuckle, Sherman, Fishback and Semnacher in Los Angeles the evening of September 9, Semnacher declared, Arbuckle expressed regret at her fate. All of the group spoke of her death as an "unfortunate accident which they could not understand," according to the witness. And Arbuckle, after a discussion of what had better be done, telephoned to the Chief of Police in San Francisco, offering to come north immediately if he was wanted.

Semnacher was the first witness to be subjected to questioning by the defense and these inquiries were but few. Aside from his statement regarding Arbuckle's conduct at the party, the defense drew from him an admission that Frank Dominguez, chief defense counsel, had told them to tell the entire truth to Captain of Detectives Duncan Matheson, and that the defense had never heard his version of the case.

The prosecution introduced as exhibits the garments, which Semnacher said Miss Rappe wore on the occasion at the St. Francis, and Dominguez asked the witness if he had seen Arbuckle wearing Ms. Rappe's Panama hat. Semnacher replied that he had not.

Brady "kids" Arbuckle

The defendant entered the courtroom with considerably more cheerfulness than he has evidenced since his arrest and grinned at District Attorney Matthew A. Brady's facetious comparison of their two waistlines. His smile died away quickly, however, as soon as the testimony began, and it did not return all morning.

Today's session of court occupied less than two hours. Women not provided with credentials were turned away from the Hall of Justice by the police, who had a much easier time of it than yesterday or the day before in handling the crowd. A corporal's guard of men spectators remained throughout the hearing, but some of the women left early. The rest of the womens' delegations from civic organizations watching the progress of the case stayed until the end, however.

After Arbuckle decided to come north to report to the San Francisco police, according to Semnacher, the start was made in the early hours of Saturday, September 10. He drove in one machine with Fishback and Sherman, while Arbuckle, Dominguez, Arbuckle's manager, Lou Anger, and the comedian's chauffeur occupied another.

There was very little discussion of Miss Rappe's death *en route*, he said, and none that involved Arbuckle's conduct with her.

[*New York Tribune*, November 29, 1921]

Comedian Gives Jury His Account of Party
Girl Lay Ill in Bathroom, Arbuckle Says
Swears Mrs. Delmont Put Ice on Head of Actress; Tells Of Drinks and Dance

(San Francisco, Nov. 28.) Roscoe ("Fatty") Arbuckle today gave on the witness stand his own version of what happened in room 1219 of the St. Francis Hotel on the fateful day when Miss Virginia Rappe met with an injury that cost her her life a few days later. Arbuckle had insisted all along that he be permitted to tell the world just what happened. His attorneys were doubtful. They feared the prosecution would tear the fat comedian's story to tatters in cross-examination. But "Fatty" prevailed over their conservatism and left the witness stand without any serious flaws having been found in his story.

<u>Arbuckle today presented himself as the victim of a chain of unfortunate circumstances</u>. Actions that had been stamped by the state as unbelievably vulgar and savage he explained as acts of mercy and chivalry. And the state, after a merciless and exhaustive examination, failed to shake him in any part of his explanation.

Found her on bathroom floor

Arbuckle's testimony was, in brief, that he did not attack Miss Virginia Rappe when he followed her into room 1219 on Labor Day and locked the door behind him; that <u>he had nothing to do with the injury that caused her death</u>. He told of unexpectedly finding the girl lying on the floor of the bathroom, writhing in pain and of ministering to her. He placed her on a bed and went to call the other women in the party. He had been in his bathrobe, pajamas and slippers all day, and had gone into the room to dress, he said, that he might go automobile riding with a friend, Mrs. Mary Taube. He had locked the door that he might not be disturbed.

Leo Friedman, Deputy District Attorney, went over and over the story with him, but failed to trip-up the defendant at any point.

Friedman's questioning had but one effect on Arbuckle – it stirred him to anger.

"Did you tell the doctor what caused Miss Rappe's illness?" Friedman demanded.

"No!" Said Arbuckle, and he half rose from his seat. "How could I tell him when I didn't know?"

Arbuckle was called to the stand early in the morning session. He looked quite solemn as he took the oath and lumbered into the chair. But when he started to answer questions he began to shift around in his seat and make gestures with his hands.

In response to questions by Gavin McNab, his chief counsel, he told how he had arisen between 10 and 11 o'clock on the morning of September 5, in his room, 1219, had bathed, shaved and put on his pajamas, his bathrobe – a handsome black plush thing lined with imperial purple – and his slippers. He was in his room about to dress when Miss Virginia Rappe entered.

"Then the others came stringing in, Miss Blake, Miss Prevost, Mrs. Delmont, Al Semnacher," he said. "I couldn't get away; I couldn't insult them and go in to dress just then.

"It was 3 o'clock when I went into room 1219. Mrs. Taube had come up about 1:30 and I told her that I had loaned my car to Fred Fishback, and that he was going out to the beach and would be back as soon as possible.

"She asked me who all these people were and I said, 'Search me. I don't know them. I didn't invite them here.' I believe, though, that I did introduce her to Miss Rappe.

"Miss Blake had to get to rehearsal at 2 o'clock. I remember looking at the clock on the mantle. I don't remember her coming back, though I remember seeing her again. Miss Rappe got up and went into room 1219. She had been sitting on the settee all afternoon. I had been sitting nearby on a chair, but I had been kidding around, dancing, eating, drinking, playing the phonograph.

"I remember distinctly it was 3 o'clock when I went into room 1219 to dress. I closed the door and locked it. I went into the bathroom.

"Miss Rappe was in the bathroom on the floor. When I opened the door, it struck her. She was ill. <u>I picked her up and carried her to 1219</u>, at her request, and placed her on a bed. She asked for water and I got her two glasses, I washed her face. I went out a minute and when I came back she was lying between the beds, having fallen off the one on which I had placed her.

"She was holding her stomach, while I held her head. I then went to 1220 to get Mrs. Delmont and the other ladies.

"I told Miss Prevost and Mrs. Delmont. <u>I asked the girls to stop her from tearing her clothes off</u>. I went into room 1219 again later and saw Miss Rappe on the bed nude. Mrs. Delmont had some ice on the back of Miss Rappe's head. I asked what the ice was doing there. Mrs. Delmont said she knew how to take care of Virginia.

"<u>I told Mrs. Delmont to shut up or I would throw her out of the window</u>. Mrs. Taube then called Mr. Boyle, the hotel manager, and a room was arranged for her.

"I put on a bathrobe and moved her to 1227.

"I never heard Virginia say 'he hurt me' or anything else that was intelligible.

"I never did have a talk with Al Semnacher about putting ice on Miss Rappe's body," the comedian declared.

He talked in a loud tone of voice and frequently arose to demonstrate his testimony.

"I never placed my hand over hers on a door in 1219," he said in reply to a question.

"No, never," he emphasized.

He then denied a conversation related by Peter Nargaard, as a state witness, in which Nargaard declared <u>Arbuckle at Culver City Studio had offered him $50 for the key to a room occupied by Miss Rappe three years ago</u>.

"I have told you everything that occurred," said Arbuckle in his final words on direct examination.

The cross examination was conducted by Assistant State District Attorney Leo Friedman.

"I have known Virginia Rappe for five or six years," he said in reply to a question by Friedman.

"We were having lunch and breakfast when Miss Prevost came.

"It was my breakfast and I drank coffee. On another table, there were gin, orange juice, White Rock and scotch whiskey. The whiskey and gin were in the closet of 1221 and Fishback brought it in. About the time, Virginia arrived.

"Miss Rappe suggested the music. She wanted a piano, but I sent for a Victrola.[8]

"We danced and drank about all afternoon until I went down to the ballroom about 8, and returned about midnight."

Asked if he had drank anything, Arbuckle said:

"Yes, sure; after breakfast I drank highballs."

Second in interest to Arbuckle's appearance on the stand was the action of the State in issuing a subpoena for Louise Glaum, noted motion picture star, and half a dozen other Hollywood personages. They are to go on the stand as rebuttal witnesses for the State.

---

[8] A popular brand of phonograph.

The first trial ended with a hung jury.

Among other headlines, this next piece shared the front page with the stories of Babe Ruth, as well as President Harding refusing an audience of delegates urging the recognition of Ireland.

[*The Evening World*, December 5, 1921]

Woman Alleges Jury Tampering In Arbuckle Case
Comedian Faces Volstead Charges Brought By US Agents

(San Francisco. Dec 5.) Collateral issues were to the fore today in the affairs of Roscoe Arbuckle, the jury which tried him on manslaughter charges having disagreed and been discharged yesterday.

Foremost of the circumstance attracting public interest was the charge made by Mrs. Helen M. Hubbard, one of the jurors who tried him on charges arising from the death of Virginia Rappe, that attempts had been made to intimidate her.

Mrs. Hubbard told Milton U'Ren, Assistant District Attorney, that a man representing himself as Gus Oliva, a commission merchant with whom her husband had had business dealings, had telephoned the husband Saturday night with the intent of having her change her vote as a juror. She let it be known that she had stood consistently for Arbuckle's conviction.

Hubbard said it had been intimated by the man that he might save himself trouble by sending his wife a note asking that she vote for Arbuckle's acquittal

Mrs. Hubbard further charged that Acting Lieutenant of Police William Lambert had attempted to communicate with her in the courtroom.

Lambert is said to be connected with Oliva in business.

All those mentioned by Mrs. Hubbard will be subpoenaed to appear before the grand jury, District Attorney Brady announced.

Mrs. Hubbard also charged that she had received fruits sent by one of the men mentioned in her intimidation while she was supposed to be locked-up at the Hotel Manx. This was confirmed by Bailiff McGovern.

Hubbard said he told Oliva that it would be impossible to get word to his wife in the locked jury room, even if he wanted to.

"I'll attend to that," he said Oliva replied. "We can send it through the Sheriff's office. They are guarding the jury room."

Actor now faces dry law accusation

The federal charge against Arbuckle, based on an allegation of illegal transportation of liquor drunk at the party in the Hotel St. Francis at which it was charged Miss Rappe had a fatal injury at Arbuckle's hands, was set for hearing today.

Charges of perjury against Mrs. Minnie Neighbors of Los Angeles, a witness called by the defense in Arbuckle's manslaughter trial, also were set for hearing today.

In addition to all these, last night's intimation by Milton Cohen, member of Arbuckle's counsel, that the defense had "something up its sleeve" and was prepared to "let it come down" today, came in for comment.

A charge that "propaganda" had been used to influence the jurors attracted much attention.

The rumors started when the bailiffs adopted the practice of changing rooms for the jury. After Saturday noon, though, two sessions were held in the same room. Many were in ignorance of exactly where the jury was meeting. Unconfirmed reports added that <u>dictaphones hidden in the walls</u> were responsible for the shift of rooms.

Arbuckle would probably leave tonight for Southern California for a few days of rest. He will then returned to San Francisco to join his lawyers in laying plans for the second trial, which will begin January 9th. He issued a statement late yesterday declaring that "one woman" on the jury had prevented a verdict in claiming that the result is a moral if not a legal acquittal. He charged that "organized propaganda designed to make the securing of an impartial jury an impossibility and to prevent my obtaining a fair trial" had been used, and he ended with this paragraph:

"I have always rested on a profound belief in divine justice and in the confidence of the great heart and fairness of the American people. I want to thank the multitude from all over the world who have telegraphed and written me in my sorrow and expressed their utmost confidence in my innocence. And I assure them that no act of mine ever has and I promise that no act of mine ever shall cause them to regret their faith in me."

"These facts speak for themselves," Arbuckle's chief counsel, Gavin McNab, declared. "Statements of counsel are superfluous."

Half-million spent by Arbuckle, is claim

District Attorney Matthew Brady was plainly pleased at the failure of Arbuckle's "million-dollar defense" to obtain an acquittal. He issued a formal statement declaring he had done his duty, "although opposed by wealth power and influence." He said he was ready to proceed January 9th with a second trial.

Brady denied claims that thousands of dollars were spent by the State.

"I believe $2,500 will cover our expenses," he said. "But say, has Arbuckle told you how much he spent?" It was rumored that the defense had cost a half million dollars.

Arbuckle, immediately after the jury was dismissed, went to his hotel with Minta Durfee, his wife, and then spent the remainder of the afternoon and evening in conference with his attorneys.

[*The Laurens Advertiser*, December 7, 1921]

Arbuckle Jury Fails To Agree
Foreman Makes Statement: Woman Juror Said She Would Cast Ballot Without Change "Till 'Hell Froze Over'"

(San Francisco, Dec. 4.) After 41 hours of deliberation, the jury, composed of seven men and five women, which tried Roscoe Arbuckle on a charge of manslaughter in connection with the death of Virginia Rappe, was discharged today when it was unable to agree upon a verdict.

The jury was brought into court at its own requests at noon, reported a disagreement and asked that it be discharged.

August Fritzie, foreman of the Arbuckle jury, issued a signed statement tonight saying that one of the women jurors who was in the minority refused to consider the evidence from the beginning and declared that "she would cast her ballot and would not change it until hell froze over."

Two for conviction

There were two jurors who voted for conviction, according to Fritzie. His statement follows:

"There was a tacit understanding that the members of the jury would not make individual statements. I have learned since that a number of the jury have, however, done so, and I believe, as foreman, that it is well for those interested in the administration of justice that the citizens of San Francisco have the facts.

"The 10 members of the jury who voted on the last ballot for acquittal felt that they voted on the evidence – fully considering it all. One of the minority refused to consider the evidence from the beginning and said, at the opening of the proceedings, that she would cast her ballot and would not change it until hell froze over. The other was fluctuating, sometimes casting the blank ballot – sometimes voting for the defense and sometimes voting for the prosecution.

"Considering all the evidence, it seemed to us that <u>the prosecution's case was an insult the intelligence of jury</u>. It asked us to substitute conjecture for facts without showing what had been done, and asked us to guess what might have been done and to guess only one way.

"Human liberty and American rights depend, not upon the guess of anybody, but upon evidence."

In a statement following the jury's return, Arbuckle declared one of the five women jurors had prevented his acquittal "because she refused to allow her fellow jurors to discuss the evidence or reason with her and would not give any reason for her attitude." He did not name the juror.

District Attorney Brady said that Arbuckle had been given a "fair and honest trial" and complemented the jurors who held out for conviction, as having "courage and determination." He was not in court when the jury reported.

"I had hoped a jury would reach an agreement," he said. "I confidently expected a verdict of guilty upon the evidence presented. In my opinion, <u>the disagreement does not vindicate Roscoe Arbuckle. A vindication would come only after a quick unanimous verdict.</u>[9] It was my duty to present the facts to a jury. This I have done, though opposed by wealth, power and influence."

Jury looked haggard

The members of the jury looked haggard and worn when they filed into the little courtroom, over which a deep hush had settled, and took their seats.

The foreman, August Fritze, informed the court "it is physically and morally impossible for us to reach a verdict." At the request of the court, he announced the final ballot division.

Superior Judge Harold Louderback, who tried the case, then told the jury he wanted to determine if further deliberation might result in a verdict. "It is not my desire to force any uncertain hardship on you," he said. "But this case has taken three weeks to try and has been conducted at great expense. If you can come to a verdict conscientiously, I desire you to do so."

He then asked each juror for an opinion on the matter of continued balloting at each answered emphatically that it would be impossible to reach a verdict.

The members of the jury refused to make statements of any kind before leaving the building. After reporting to the court, they were escorted to a side street by deputy sheriffs and taken to their homes and automobiles.

"While this, through technicalities of the law, is not a legal acquittal, morally it is such," Arbuckle said in discussing the jury's inability to agree.

---

[9] Prescient of the third trial described beginning on page 105.

"The undisputed and uncontradicted testimony established that my only connection with the sad affair was of a merciful service and the fact that ordinary human kindness should have brought upon me this tragedy has seemed a cruel wrong," his statement continued.

"I have sought to bring joy and gladness and merriment into the world and why this great misfortune should have fallen upon me is a mystery that only God can and will someday reveal."

After stating that he rested his cause "in divine justice and the confidence of the fairness of the American people," Arbuckle concluded with the declaration that "no action of mine ever has, and I promise that no action of mine ever shall, cause them to regret their faith in me."

Arbuckle's defense was that he was assisting Miss Rappe through a period of illness, caused, according to defense contentions, by an internal disorder at the time is alleged by the prosecution to have injured her.

<u>The prosecution held that the injury resulted from attempt by Arbuckle to attack the actress</u>.

U'Ren said that Mrs. Hubbard told him the bailiff who had charge of the jury, and a number of reporters, that two men approached her husband, T. W. Hubbard, with a view to have him use his influence to have her change her vote.

Charges that attempts were made to intimidate Mrs. Helen M. Hubbard, juror in the Roscoe Arbuckle manslaughter trial, will be laid before the grand jury tomorrow night, it was announced late tonight by Milton U'Ren, Assistant District Attorney.

Mrs. Hubbard let it be known that she had been voting for a verdict of guilty on the manslaughter charge whereof the motion picture comedian was accused.

[*Bridgeport Times and Evening Farmer*, January 9, 1922]

Fatty Arbuckle Goes On Trial for Second Time
Famous Movie Actor Must Again Face Ordeal of Fighting To Free Himself of the Manslaughter Charge Resulting From Death of Virginia Rappe

(San Francisco, Jan. 9.) For a second time Roscoe ("Fatty") Arbuckle, famous funster of the silver screen, went on trial today for manslaughter. He is charged with responsibility for the death of Virginia Rappe, film actress, who died following a gay hotel party given by Arbuckle here September 5.

His first trial, following a bitter legal battle, ended in disagreement on the part of the jury, the last ballot having stood ten to two for acquittal.

An entire new jury venire[10] was drawn for the opening of the second trial today before judge Harold Louderback.

As in the first trial, District Attorney Matthew Brady was in court to personally direct the prosecution of the State's case, with Milton U'Ren and Leo Friedman as his chief assistants.

Arranged on the side of the bulky comedian, as in his first trial, where Gavin McNab, chief of counsel; Nath Schmulowitz, Charles H. Brennan, Milton Cohen and Joseph McInerny, associate counsel.

Opinion differed as the second trial opened as to the length of time that would be required to complete the case.

"I do not believe it will take as long as the first trial," said McNab.

"I don't believe the trial will be any shorter than the first, and maybe it will take longer," said District Attorney Brady.

---

[10] Jury pool

<u>The first trial lasted about three weeks.</u>

The selection of a jury is expected to take up the greater part of this week, with the taking of evidence getting underway about Friday.

Both sides have been active during the period intervening between the two trials. It is not believed that either State or defense has uncovered any startling new evidence, but both sides profess to have found cumulative evidence to assist their case.

The defense claims to have found a number of witnesses who testified to <u>the alleged propensity of Miss Rappe to tear her clothing when drinking</u> and that she was subject to a chronic trouble which caused her violent paroxysms of pain at frequent intervals. On the other hand, the State claims to have witnesses whose testimony will throw discredit on this claim of the defense.

There were also indications that the defense planned to launch a savage attack on fingerprint evidence introduced by the State at the first trial. It is the contention of the State that Miss Rappe came to injuries that caused her death while alone in room 1219 with Arbuckle, at the St. Francis Hotel.

They introduced into evidence the door leading from room 1219 to 1220 and, through Dr. E. O. Heinrichs, showed finger marks which he identified as those of Arbuckle, superimposed over those of Miss Rappe. At the first trial due to legal rulings, the defense was unable to get their fingerprint experts on the stand. At this trial, they will present an entirely new set of experts whose qualifications will ensure their being able to testify. At the same time, it is understood, the qualifications of Heinrichs will be attacked. It is probable that the defense will make a strenuous battle to keep the fingerprint testimony out altogether.

As in the first trial, the State will rely on Alice Blake and Zey Prevost, showgirls who attended the party, as star witnesses.

Although interest is not as high as in the first trial[11] it was apparent today that the capacity of the small courtroom will again be taxed to accommodate the crowds anxious to hear the testimony.

[*Carson City Appeal*, Feb 3, 1922]

Arbuckle Jury, Standing 10 - 2 for Conviction, Discharged

(San Francisco, Cal., Feb. 3.) The jury trying Roscoe (Fatty) Arbuckle on a charge of manslaughter growing out of the death of Miss Virginia Rappe was discharged at 11:30 o'clock this morning after many hours deliberation. The final vote stood 10 to 2 for conviction.

The District Attorney gave notice shortly before the jury was discharged that if he did not secure a conviction by the jury he would not prosecute Arbuckle again, on account of the heavy expense.

Attorney Gavin McNab, chief counsel for Arbuckle, announced that the defense would insist upon a third trial for the vindication of the film comedian. His statement was as follows:

"Regardless of what the District Attorney may have in mind, the counsel for Roscoe Arbuckle will insist that we proceed to another trial immediately.

"I wish to add also that we are prepared to leave no stone unturned to present a much fuller array of facts than have been offered to the public at the first two

---

[11] Indeed, progress in the case, from arrest through just prior to the eventual acquittal, moved from the front-page inwards.

proceedings. We shall ask the court to fix a date for the next trial just as soon as this jury is dismissed, in the event of a mistrial."

[*Mt. Sterling Advocate*, February 7, 1922]

Arbuckle Jury Is Discharged

The jury in the second trial of the manslaughter charge against Roscoe C. Arbuckle decided at the conclusion of a 44-hour session that it would not agree and was discharged at San Francisco Friday, with the final ballot standing 10 to 2 for conviction.

Arbuckle was accused of having caused the death of Virginia Rappe of Los Angeles, a motion picture actress who was taken ill at a drinking party at the Hotel St. Francis on Labor Day, 1921, and died four days later of a ruptured bladder.

So sure was the defense of its position in a second trial that it had submitted its case without final arguments. This had an effect opposite from the one intended, according to Nate Friedman, one of the jurors, in a formal statement.

"We thought that when the defense declined to argue, it had thrown up its hands," he said. "The first 10 ballots stood 9 to 3 for conviction, and thereafter, until the 14th and final ballot, it was 10 to 2 for conviction."

Arbuckle appeared to be somewhat downcast by the disagreement. Members of his family were visibly perturbed.

The jury was out one hour longer than the jury in the first trial, which had announced a final ballot of 10 to 2 for acquittal.

The jurors looked haggard and worn, and the woman juror, Mrs. Mary H. Somers, was visibly nervous. The crowded courtroom heard the result.

"In spite of my personal conviction, it was my intent to be guided by the opinion of the majority of the jury," District Attorney Brady said. "Had the majority of the jury been in favor of an acquittal I would have asked for a dismissal. As the jury stood 10 for conviction to two for acquittal, it is manifestly my duty to try the case again."

Gavin McNab, chief counsel for Arbuckle, issued the following statement:

"The jury in the first trial, on practically all ballots, stood 11 for acquittal and one alternate for acquittal and one juryman for conviction.

"In this trial, on practically all ballots, the jury stood nine for conviction and three for acquittal, with the two alternates for acquittal.

"Practically the same evidence was presented to each jury. The case will be tried again by a third jury. We, who know that Arbuckle is innocent, are confident that truth will prevail."

Virginia Rappe. *Library of Congress.*

[*Great Falls Tribune*, April 13, 1922]

Jury Acquits Arbuckle, Verdict Hailed
Injustice Done Actor Say Jurors after Six Minutes Taken To Free
American People Asked In Statement to Accept Finding as Insufficient Vindication; Wife Weeps and Kisses Counsel McNab; Arbuckle Holds Reception with 12 Who Decided Case

A statement issued by the Arbuckle jury, signed by all the jurors, including the two alternates, declares:

"Acquittal is not enough for Roscoe Arbuckle.

"We feel that a great injustice has been done him. We feel also that it was only our plain duty to give him this exoneration, under the evidence, for there was not the slightest proof adduced to connect him in any way with the commission of a crime.

"He was manly throughout the case and told a straightforward story on the witness stand, which we all believed.

"The happening at the hotel was an unfortunate affair for which Arbuckle, so the evidence shows, was in no way responsible.

"We wish him success and hope that the American people will take the judgment of 14 men and women who have sat listening for 31 days to the evidence, that Roscoe Arbuckle is entirely innocent and free from all blame."

(San Francisco, April 12.) A verdict of acquittal was returned by a jury today in the third trial of Roscoe C. (Fatty) Arbuckle, on a manslaughter charge growing out of the death of Miss Virginia Rappe, motion picture actress.

The jury was out six minutes.

The defendant was deeply affected. The verdict was received by him with a great sigh of relief. There was no demonstration, the court having warned against it.

Mrs. Minta Durfee, the defendant's wife, cried quietly. Both she and Arbuckle shook hands with the jurors. Mrs. Arbuckle expressed her thanks to McNab by giving him a resounding kiss.

The quick return of the jury was a surprise. The verdict was by acclamation, <u>the deliberation taking less than a minute</u>. The additional time was consumed by details.

The jurors and spectators crowded around Arbuckle and his counsel and finally bore him off to the jury room to congratulate him further.

The jurors held an informal reception with Arbuckle in the jury room, while newspaper photographers armed with flashlights took many pictures.

Both sides waived the reading of written instructions in the court's final charge to the jury. The courtroom was packed throughout the final session.

By coincidence, the case went to the jury at approximately the same time as in the two former hearings, which ended in disagreements.

The day was occupied largely by the concluding argument of Gavin McNab, chief counsel for the defense, and Leo Friedman, youthful Assistant District Attorney. McNab charged that the District Attorney "processed" witnesses to "railroad" Arbuckle to the penitentiary. Answering this, Friedman said that had the prosecution attempted to "frame the case" there would have been no chance for the defense.

Arbuckle was nervous throughout Friedman's arguments. He whispered to his counsel at times when Friedman appeared to make a particularly telling point.

The third trial of the manslaughter charge against Arbuckle began March 6, and was marked by the appearance of approximately <u>70 witnesses</u> and the calling of two of the defense witnesses before the county grand jury in connection with their testimony. The trial was longer than either of the previous hearings of the case, consuming nearly five weeks.

[*South Bend News Time*, April 13, 1922]

Comedian Freed In Record Time by Jury
Medical Testimony Keynote

As in the previous hearings, much emphasis was placed on expert medical testimony regarding the exact condition of Miss Rappe's bladder before and after death. This testimony was based on an autopsy finding that Miss Rappe came to her death from the rupture. The prosecution presented a report by a commission of three pathologists appointed at the first trial purporting to show that, while the organ appeared to have been slightly inflamed, this irregularity did not predispose it to rupture.

The defense evidence was of the effect that Miss Rappe came to her death as a result of the sudden crisis in a chronic illness, which led to a rupture.

Witnesses subpoenaed to appear before the grand jury were Mrs. Virginia Warren, a nurse, and Mrs. Helen Madelyne Whitehurst, both of Chicago. Mrs. Warren, a new witness, <u>testified that she attended Miss Rappe in Chicago on one occasion when the girl gave birth to a baby</u>[12]. Mrs. Whitehurst repudiated a deposition which she admitted signing in Chicago to the effect that she had seen Miss Rappe ill on a number of occasions at the girl's home. She expressed the belief that the deposition was altered after she had signed it and it was introduced into testimony as an altered document.

---

[12] This revelation seems to accomplish little more than impugning Rappe's character as promiscuous.

[*Capital Journal*, April 14, 1922]
Three Trials Cost Arbuckle Over $110,000

(San Francisco, Cal., April 14.) The defense of Roscoe C Arbuckle in the three manslaughter trials in connection with the death of Miss Virginia Rappe, <u>cost more than $110,000, not including attorney's fees</u>,[13] it was learned here today. The bringing of witnesses from Chicago and other distant points entail the greatest portion of this expense.

It is the plan to release all of Arbuckle's films which were completed at the time he met with his difficulties in San Francisco. This will be done gradually. The comedian himself has not perfected his future plans, but according to those close to him, these lay between returning to the screen as an actor and directing the production of films.

Arbuckle was asked to present a monologue between pictures by two of the biggest motion picture theaters here after his acquittal Wednesday, but declined to do so. He explained his refusal with the statement:

"I do not care to capitalize my good fortune so soon after achieving it. There is a sentiment attached to the experience of acquittal that must come before any commercialism. I will return to my profession when I consider it proper to do so."

---

[13] A separate unverified report claimed Arbuckle owed his legal team $700,000. His total defense, then, in 2018 dollars, cost him $12.2 million. Compare that to the cost of O. J. Simpson's defense and "Dream Team," estimated in 2018 dollars, to be between $5M and $8.25M!

And the Other Matter

[*The Washington Herald*, October 8, 1921]
Hand of Law Taps Fatty Once More
Obese Arbuckle Arrested on Volstead Charge

(**San Francisco, Oct. 7.**) Roscoe Arbuckle, the corpulent movie comedian, had a new trouble to worry about today.

He came here today for arraignment on a charge of having caused the death of Virginia Rappe.

But just as he stepped from the courtroom after his arraignment had been postponed, and ordered a taxi to take him to his brother's home, a prohibition agent stepped up and told him that he had violated the Volstead law.

"That so?" inquired Fatty.

"Yes," mumbled the agent, "and you are under arrest."

Fatty's face said: "Well, that's nothing new," but he made no actual remark and accompanied the officer to the United States Commissioner's Court, where he was released on $500 bond.

> **FATTY'S $25,000 CAR; DRY AGENTS WILL RIDE IN IT**
>
> Roscoe Arbuckle's custom-built automobile, equipped with every convenience, from a cellaret [*liquor cabinet*] to instruments telling its altitude—not to mention 20 bottles of whiskey alleged to have been transported in it from Los Angeles to Frisco.
>
> **(Los Angeles, Calif., Sept. 16)** More than forty quarts of liquor were consumed in the three-day party in Roscoe (Fatty) Arbuckle's suite in a San Francisco hotel, which preceded the death of Miss Virginia Rappe, according to information given federal officers here by Frederick Fishback, a member of the party. This was announced today by Robert Camarillo, Assistant United States Attorney.
>
> Fishback's statement, which was taken down by a stenographer, was given in the presence of Mr. Camarillo, E. Forest Mitchell, Federal Prohibition Director for California, and other federal officials, according to Mr. Camarillo.
>
> Twenty bottles of whisky, Mr. Camarillo stated Fishback told them, were taken in Arbuckle's car from Los Angeles to San Francisco; and while he was at the hotel, a case of gin was taken to Arbuckle's suite by a "tall thin man" and other liquor by "a dark stranger."
>
> The home of Lowell Sherman, another member of the Arbuckle party, was visited by the federal officials seeking further data.
>
> They stated that if Fishback's declarations were sustained, Arbuckle's automobile, said to be valued at $25,000, would be confiscated under the terms of the Volstead Act.
>
> —*The Rock Island Argus and Daily Union*,
> September 16, 1921

Arbuckle's arrest today marks the first actual move in the liquor investigation launched by Special Assistant United States Attorney Robert McCormick, who announced his intention of prosecuting everyone who had a hand in furnishing liquor for Arbuckle's famous Labor Day party, which proceeded to death of Miss Rappe.

Arbuckle's arraignment in court was brief, the time for pleading being put over until October 13.

"October 13 is a hoodoo day," the court clerk commented.

"No, no one of us cares," spoke up Charles Brennan of Arbuckle's counsel. "There's nothing unlucky about this case."

Regrettably, no mention in reports was made of the final disposition of the charge though one account reported Arbuckle was fined $500, the amount of his bail on the charge.

A NIFTY LITTLE "SUBMARINE," BUT IT SAILS GASOLINE TRAIL, NOT WAR ZONE

VIRGINIA RAPPE

The dirt and dust of the gasoline trail have no terrors for the girl who motors—not if she wears a "submarine bonnet."

The "submarine bonnet" is new—it made its debut in the Sunday procession on Lake Shore drive, when Miss Virginia Rappe, the artist whose hobby is designing artistic "things to wear," appeared in her car in a "submarine bonnet."

"Women usually wear their ugliest things when they go a-motoring," said Miss Rappe when she showed me the little bonnet that looks so much like the helmet of a submarine diver. "But this bonnet of mine fits so snugly around the face that it makes a pretty frame and improves even a face that isn't pretty. It covers head and neck completely and protects one from every speck of dust.

"I used brown taffeta in my 'submarine' and this little apple that dangles above my eye is quite trimming enough. .The hood opens at the back and it fastens with hooks."

From *The Day Book*, **June 10, 1915.**

Commentary

Predictably, there was no shortage of opinion on the Arbuckle case and/or the verdict.

The 1922 Medico-Legal Journal, for instance, focused on the evidence citing the plausibility of a "homicide by misadventure." The likelihood of Rappe's bladder rupture at Arbuckle's hands (or rather his 266 pounds), they wrote, is "a possibility rendered much easier if the female be recumbent and with the thighs flexed or partially so upon the abdomen... unless surgical intervention is early, the injury is almost uniformly fatal from peritonitis."

One of the more interesting commentaries on the trial is this one from the March/April 1922 issue of the Communist publication, The Young Worker. *It should be remembered that the Communist Revolution occurred only a few years prior.*

The Morals of the Movies
A Review of the Arbuckle Case

Moving pictures are one of the most powerful propaganda forces wielded by the capitalistic class. To the millions of people who daily go to the picture shows is doled out the "virtues" of capitalism. The master class does not overlook any opportunity to slander organized labor through the use of pictures. And a philosophy that is disseminated by use of the serene (sugar-coated with humor) is calculated to "appease" the hungry and to feed the unemployed with hope.

Because of their plastic minds, the young are especially apt to derive "instruction" from the pictures. The children and young people of this country attend the picture shows more frequently than do the adults. Hence the propaganda reaches them and to a greater degree.

The morals of capitalism as portrayed by such actors as "Fatty" Arbuckle and the countless number of his type who have not had the misfortune to have committed so slight an error as murder are set up as examples to the future generation.

Accidents will happen; and once in a generation a cog will slip in the well-regulated machine and we get a glimpse of the true character of these teachers of morality

But the capitalists will not desert so "valuable" a man as "Fatty" and they begin to pull the strings to acquit him. <u>Incidentally, the impartiality of our justice-dispensing machinery is revealed in all its hideousness</u>.

It is easier to observe the actions of others. And the following interesting analysis of the Arbuckle case and justice in the United States gives us a picture of a phase of American capitalism as seen by our English comrades.

(From the *British Communist*.)

So Roscoe – "Fatty" – Arbuckle is to come to trial again. Arbuckle was not always a rich man, he was once a "saloon bum," a down-and-out hangar-on of pubs. As a chucker-out and as a potboy he once earned a more or less honest living, until he struck lucky on the films. But even in his time of great wealth he retained the manners and habits of his pub crawling days. He is, or was, at least, before this action began, a millionaire, and behind him are many of the most important cinema firms of the U.S.A. who have some miles of Arbuckle films which they dare not release 'till the fat comedian is acquitted

District Attorney Brady, of California, prosecuting him, exclaimed:

"Can you tell me how I can join a bomb-throwing organization? I mean an organization more violent than the I.W.W.?[14] I believe in dynamiting when I see such efforts to pervert justice!"

District Attorney Brady is not a strong man. He is a weak and uncertain man, but he was put into office largely by a Labor vote, to perform one definite duty – to dislocate the whole operation of the "Frame-up" ring of California.

This Ring originally worked through Brady's predecessor, Fickert. It used him to jail for life a San Francisco Labor leader, Tom Mooney,[15] on a false charge of dynamiting. It produced forged evidence and suppressed real evidence. Witness after witness was brought forward and torn to pieces, and their places at once cynically taken by other hired agents. Eventually Mooney was condemned to death, but the grossness of the fraud was such that the sentence was changed to imprisonment for life – and he is still in jail.

For capitalist justice in California has gone one step further than it has here. There it is completely corrupt and completely at the direct service of a financial ring who owns all the judges, can interfere in the selection of jurors, and has a regular service of false witnesses for use

---

[14] The socialist organization *Industrial Workers of the World*.

[15] One of two (the other being Warren Billings) convicted in the July, 1916 Preparedness Day Bombing in San Francisco. Ten were killed when a bomb exploded at a parade celebrating (?!) the U.S. entrance into WWI.

in almost any case. The utter filthiness of this whole gang was bound to provoke a reaction, and when Fickert was found to be having dealings with the Germans an opportunity arose for the election of a substitute – Brady – who was pledged to their destruction.

The Frame-up ring has now been called-in to defend Arbuckle, and it is defeating Brady. It has been called in because Arbuckle is essential to the California anti-union forces. He is the biggest propagandist inside the cinema trade for the "open shop" campaign which is now being pressed hard. A strong and partly-successful attempt has been made to smash unionism in the film trade (an "open shop" is a non-union shop) and cut wages. The twelve firms involved in this drive are:

Christie Film Co., Thos. H. Ince Productions, Hal E. Roach Studios, Brunton Studios Inc., Buster Keaton Comedies, Lasky-Famous Players Co., Metro Pictures Corp., William Fox Studios, Goldwyn Pictures Corp., Realart Pictures Corp., Universal Film Company.

<u>Fatty Arbuckle, their star scab actor</u>, was also their best assets in this campaign. And then he gets himself arrested for rape and murder.

Still, money can do most things and the Frame-up ring got busy.

First of all Judge Lazarus was made to reduce the charge from <u>one of murder by rape to manslaughter</u>. It will be remembered that Arbuckle carried the girl, Virginia Rappe, out of the room at a drunken party in his hotel saying, "I've waited for you five years;" that a chambermaid passing by the bedroom door heard the girl's screams and struggles; that the guests who entered the room later found her naked and an agony crying, "He hurt me!" while Arbuckle, dressed in the girl's picture hat, stood by saying, "If she screams again, I'll throw her out of the window."

Virginia Rappe died of the injuries he had inflicted.

At the trial, the Frame-up ring got hold of one witness after another and "persuaded" them that they had perjured themselves. It went far afield to search out means of throwing mud at the dead girl's character. It saw to it that Judge Lazarus summed up as heavily as he could against the prosecution, describing the chambermaid as "hysterical," and laying the greatest stress upon the points put forward by the more-than-shady witnesses for the defense. And the papers were able to announce that Fatty was "morally acquitted" because the jury was 10 to 2 for acquittal.

But the California bosses don't leave such things as juror's votes to the chances of evidence. The jury was selected in advance, at least in the majority, and its foreman, Fritze, was a well-known agent of the ring. The juror who stood out for conviction, Mrs. Helen Hubbard, now publicly swears that Fritze and others' threats of violence and intimidation, also third degree methods, forced her to agree to acquittal. Fritze used to her the words, "I'll knock your __ __ block off!" Her husband, T.W. Hubbard, was approached by one of the ring (a minor member, Oliva) demanding that he instruct his wife to vote for acquittal. Oliva further said that he (Oliva) would pass the note through to the jury, and that if Hubbard refused, he would be ruined.

That is trial by jury in California.

But the Frame-up ring goes deeper in the mire than that. How did this honest woman, Mrs. Helen Hubbard, find herself on that jury? The Frame-up ring had "double-crossed" Fatty. It knew he could be bled for more money and intended that he should have to stand a second trial.

That is United States' Justice. It was that same Frame-up ring which condemned Tom Mooney to imprisonment for life on an utterly false charge five years ago – and he is still in jail. It is that same system of justice which has now forged a whole case against two Italian-American active trade unionists – Sacco and Vanzetti[16] – and condemned them to death on an equally false charge.

Tom Mooney's Monthly writes:

"Fatty" Arbuckle and motion pictures are inseparable – the Frameup ring knows this and it is bent on a rich harvest. It knew in advance just what the verdict would be in the Arbuckle trial. Vincent Riccardi[17] exposed this feature of the Frameup ring's work last year when he showed, beyond any doubt, the methods of control and the uses to which the Ring put this so-called machinery of justice to work for its own enrichment.

Riccardi showed that it was the sworn policy of the Ring to have disagreements where its victim (the defendant) had not been shaken down for all of his money. If the Ring knew he had more money or opportunities of obtaining it, it would split the jury by placing upon it those who it knew in advance would vote not to agree on a verdict. Some regular acquitters and some regular convicters – thus does it produce a mistrial and open-up another avenue to the pockets of "Fatty" and his rich friends.

Now should "Fatty" and his rich friends in the scab, open-shop, 100% "American" plan motion picture enterprises come clean with enough coin of the realm between

---

[16] Nicola Sacco and Bartolomeo Vanzetti were anarchists convicted (and executed) for an armed robbery.

[17] Riccardi had confessed on another occasion to having fixed juries claiming to expose the corruption in the judicial process.

now and the time for the next trial, he will never be brought to trial; the case will be dismissed "for lack of sufficient evidence to convict."

If he fails to dig up the "dough" in large sums, the Frameup ring will hold the club of another trial over his head and make him come across with many dollars or the big gates of San Quentin prison will await him. In fact, it would not surprise us to see a second disagreement.[18] It would mean more thousands of dollars in the coffers of the Ring.

Most times we think very little of the pious resolutions and hardly annuals which are passes regularly by Labor Party and Trades Union Congresses. But we do think this time that it would be a crime to fail to make at least a verbal protest. The friends who are defending Sacco and Vanzetti, the friends who are still seeking the release of Mooney, specifically ask for protest by the British workers, believing that over there, these will have some effect. We must not refuse them.

As for Fatty, we can do little to express our contempt of him and his defenders. "Union Labor is through with Fatty's pictures," says *Tom Mooney's Monthly*, from America: we suppose, too, that it will be long before a decent working man, or his wife or kids, wastes another ninepence over here on the fat beast.

---

[18] The second trial did, indeed, fail to either convict or acquit.

This opinion from Winnifred Black, "noted writer on women's affairs" focused on declining morals, a post-WWI trend, apparently.

Three life tragedies show decay of moral instinct in young girls

Dead, in misery and disgrace!
Dead, in shame and humiliation!
Dead, in agony and despair!
Olive Thomas – in Paris![19]
"Billie" Carleton – in London![20]
Virginia Rappe – in San Francisco!
Three young, beautiful girls, full of life and the joy of living!

And every one of them died in a way that would have made the mother who bore them wish they had strangled them in their cradles if she could have looked ahead and envisioned even dimly the horror that came to them!

What does it all mean – where is it all going to end?

This girl who died in San Francisco the other day in hideous agony has never been connected in any way with any scandalous stories of disgraceful parties before.

She was a quiet, well behaved, modest girl, they say, intelligent and well enough accustomed to the ways of the world to know what "wild parties" meant.

How did she happen to go to such an orgy, and after she got there, when she found out the sort of "party" it was, why didn't she leave the place immediately?

---

[19] A film actress poisoned in Paris in 1920.
[20] An English actress rumored to have overdosed in London in 1919.

Virginia Rappe. *Library of Congress.*

What was a self-respecting proud, high-hearted girl doing at such a place?

Just exactly what hundreds and perhaps even thousands of other girls are doing day-in and day-out, and night-in and night-out, all over this country.

The old-fashioned rules that protected girls who had not sense enough to protect themselves have all been broken.

Ten years ago, the girl who would go to a man's room in a hotel, party or no party, would have thrown away her good name the instant the fact of her visit was known.

Ten years ago, any woman who stayed for 10 minutes in a room with a half-drunken man would have been considered no better than the man.

Ten years ago, girls of decent reputation did not frequent the company of men who were known to be shameless and disgusting brutes.

<u>Since the war all this is changed</u>.

All defenses are down, all the rules are "back numbers,"[21] and half the girls we meet in the street and see at the theater and know in the homes of our best friends are subjected day after day to dangers of which their mothers never dream of.

All over the world, the situation is nothing less than appalling, and in America it is worse than anywhere else.

Everybody who knows anything about Arbuckle or his kind at all ought to know what a "party" given by him will mean.

But he is rich; he owns a $25,000 automobile and has, goodness knows, how many servants and valets and hangers-on of every description.

Besides, he's a celebrity.

---

[21] No longer popular.

Arbuckle's stepmother doesn't hold back in this next report describing his early days. The reader can decide if it is mere background or an attempt at rationalizing Arbuckle's later behavior.

[*Arizona Republican*, September 26, 1921]

Stepmother Arbuckle "Forgot"
Tells of Fatty's Boyhood Days

(Santa Clara, Calif.) This is a "cut back," in film parlance, from the tragic Virginia Rappe episode in Roscoe Arbuckle's life reel to a "close-up" of his boyhood as pic-pictured by the aged stepmother who has long felt herself renounced by him.

The location is a humble home on the outskirts of this California town where Mrs. Molly Arbuckle, 63, and lifelong breadwinner over the washtubs, paused with folded hands to recite her story of "Fatty's" lugubrious amble toward fame.

When as a widow with five children she married Roscoe's father, with four, Mrs. Arbuckle mothered the boy through adolescence.

She speaks with tender pity of his seriocomic youth when the poundage that was to make him celebrated served but as a target for the village jibes.

She tells of his chronic laziness; of his unhappy days at school; of her unavailing efforts to stir his ambition, pride of person and industry.

And then she directs the spotlight out along the road to fortune taken by this puzzling lad who trudged it with a loaf and a laugh; tells of his failure to write, his forgetfulness of the mixed family with whom he grew up, and his indifference to her increased burdens when the husband deserted the double brood.

"But it is no more than I expected of Roscoe," she states unemotionally, with neither bitterness nor reproach.

"He was aggravatingly lazy as a boy. Neither his father's cuffings[22] nor my pleadings could cure. He didn't do any work around the house and didn't contribute towards the family support, though his truthful brothers did their full share.

"Roscoe was a big, fat boy who weighed 16 pounds at birth. He didn't seem to fit in anywhere very well. He quit school in the fifth grade before I married his father. I urged him to go back, but Mr. Arbuckle was indifferent. And when he did start, his father compelled him to wear these old overalls and shabby shoes so that the schoolchildren jeered him. That hurt Roscoe and he stayed away for longer and longer periods, spending his time near the river fishing and in solitude, finally quitting altogether. I was sorry for him.

"His father used to beat him – and I will say he often deserved it.

"One of his brothers secured him a job and two weeks' board and room at a hotel for him. His untidiness made him an object of reproach there.

"Then he started hanging around saloons, finally getting work as a bar boy, cleaning the floors. He would jig-step half an hour for a mug of beer and at such times, oddly enough, he seemed to have plenty of energy.

"When he left Santa Clara he owed a number of people small amounts. One was a working girl from whom he borrowed $2.50 the night he went away. And she is still hopeful of its repayment. I suppose he has forgotten – as he forgot us.

---

[22] Beatings.

"He has never written to me or any of the family. Often he has driven through the town in his fine automobile but he never seems to find time to stop and say hello or to recognize his folks. The only way we learn what he is doing is through the papers.

"No, I have never gone to see him in the movies. I am not without my pride, and if he wants none of us, so let be."

Mrs. Arbuckle recounted how he was on stage in song and dance at the old Unique Theater in San Jose, then with the Ferris Hartman stock company as a comedian, later to the Orient, and then back to California with Mack Sennett as an extra man in motion pictures.

"I pity the boy," she resumed speaking quietly. "I hope he is not guilty of that dreadful thing, but if he is, I would see him punished.

"I have been told that Roscoe now intends sending me some money. But I will not touch it. I feel it would not come to me unprompted and I should return it."

Deep affection, it seems, never grew up between Arbuckle and his stepmother, though there was no antagonism. Other members of the family show some resentment at fate rather than at their kinsman for the queer twist that brought him opulence out of slothfulness while they have but a mere living for their steady plodding.

This feeling the stepmother shows no sign of sharing, although there is striking contrast between her humble estate in Santa Clara and the sumptuous $100,000 home of Roscoe Arbuckle in Los Angeles with its creamy $25,000 auto in the garage.

If "Fatty" has risen to eminence with a loaf and a laugh, they have been a battle and a march. When she married Arbuckle, she says, he was managing a restaurant in Santa Clara. She helped him there as well as doing the home work. She paid the home rent, she avers, and all the family expenses, and proudly treasures the receipted bills. She feels she was born to toil, and for her husband's vagaries, as she recites them, there is no resentment. Only she resents and indignantly denies reports that Arbuckle, the father, was a drunkard.

Unlike the palatial home of her famous stepson, Mrs. Arbuckle's house is lighted with kerosene lamps and has few modern conveniences. She carries the water from a well-formed washtub — still her method of livelihood, supplemented by aid from her other sons now all grown. On the clean floors are rag carpets of her own weaving. One of her two daughters helps with housework. They are not blind, as has been reported.

Molly Arbuckle is proud of toil, gives much, asks little for herself, and has battled the way for her brood without complaint.

"They are all poor," she says of her family. "And they have all helped — except Roscoe."

Tolerant of his other characteristics, whether she approves them or not, Roscoe Arbuckle's stepmother reasons only his renunciation of the family. That pricks her unbending pride and self-respect.

If his former admirers are veering in his hour of trouble she sees in that a sign of retribution.

Thus the "cut back" fades, the reel again picks up the frowning comedian in the cell of San Francisco's city prison and proceeds to unwind through gruesome inquest details and grand jury testimony toward the trial for the death of Virginia Rappe with which Roscoe "Fatty" Arbuckle is charged.

The Holly Leaves, *a neighborhood publication, was not quite ready to accept Arbuckle's innocence but is willing to, "for the sake of argument." From their December 29, 1922, issue:*

For Sake of the Argument

For the sake of the argument, we are willing to admit that Fatty Arbuckle had no part in the death of Virginia Rappe.

For the sake of the argument, we are willing to admit that Arbuckle never was any worse in his private life than many another man in and out of pictures.

For the sake of the argument, we are willing to admit that Arbuckle is genuinely repentant of his former evil ways and is now our reformed man – as pure as the driven snow.

For the sake of the argument, we are willing to admit that Arbuckle films have always been refined and of uplifting character.

We have serious doubts on all these points but we are willing to admit them FOR THE SAKE OF THE ARGUMENT.

BUT that does not alter the fact that the details of Arbuckle's former life as brought out in the Rappe trials has made his name a synonym for the most disgusting debauchery. Everywhere today, Arbuckle's name, with its unsavory associations, is met with a sneer. Everywhere indecent living is branded as "Fatty Arbuckle stuff." It is impossible to speak his name or to see his picture without connecting him with his nasty record. His return to the screen would mean keeping of all this filth continually before the public by suggestion and association.

We contend that no man can be innocent enough, or reformed enough, to make such a flaunting and disreputable past before the youth of the land warranted or excusable.

The "chance" that Arbuckle should ask for in these days of his alleged reformation is not the chance to get back into the limelight but the chance to work out his salvation quietly in seclusion, forgotten by those whose trusting friendliness in former days he's so foully betrayed.

The additional "exoneration" of Arbuckle by the [3rd] jury that acquitted him always seemed to us a bit gratuitous anyhow. Such consideration was most unusual, to say the least. It would be interesting and enlightening to know on whose suggestion and by whose persuasion these 12 men and women went out of their way to pronounce such an uncalled for *obiter dictum*.[23] In our opinion, the situation would bear a little investigation.

Who killed cock Robin?

Will Hays[24] says he has not reinstated Arbuckle in the films. Perhaps Mr. Hays did not banish Arbuckle from the films some months ago. But if Hays didn't who did? The little Napoleon was glad enough to take the credit for the first act. Why should he seek to sidestep the blame for the second.

---

[23] An incidental remark

[24] Hays was the first chairman of the Motion Picture Producers and Distributors of America which introduced a movie morals "code" outlining, for example, which words, acts and themes were taboo. Films produced before these 1930 guides were introduced are referred to as "pre-code."

The public outranks Hays

Will Hays will find that there is higher authority than he in the motion picture world. He will get his reprimand in the Arbuckle case from the box office.

Eastern papers please copy

Every Hollywood newspaper has denounced the plan to return Arbuckle to films <u>If you want an inside view of the ideals and temper of Hollywood, here it is</u>.

This is our last shot

Mr. Hays is evidently suffering from "Fatty" degeneration of the heart.

Billy Sunday, the popular evangelist of the early 20th century, seemingly blamed the victim, though a closer read clearly places the blame on demon rum.

[*The Washington Times*, September 18, 1921]

Let "Fatty" Go, Girl guilty
by Billy Sunday

(Sioux City, Iowa, Sept. 17.) I feel sorry for "Fatty" Arbuckle and do not see how any court in the land could convict the fallen idol for murder or for manslaughter. He has suffered enough, in my opinion.

How can you punish Arbuckle unless you punish Mrs. Bambina Maude Delmont and the others who were his guests at the St. Francis and who have told their story to District Attorney Brady?

I blame booze for the whole thing. Had there been no liquor at that party, Virginia Rappe would not have lost her life. But there were intoxicants and I see by the papers that forty quarts of whiskey and other hard liquor was consumed by "Fatty" and his guests.

Now his pictures are barred. And while they are banning his pictures they should quit showing Miss Rappe's.

Without a doubt, she went to that party of her own free will and accord.

From what I gather from the papers, Miss Rappe also went into the bedroom with "Fatty," not because he forced her to go, for it seems that he did not, but because she wanted to go in there with him.

The girl died, but I believe her death was caused by an accident and not by Roscoe Arbuckle.

Probably the most bizarre, and seemingly anti-Semitic, view of the trial conclusion is this one from the February 11, 1922 issue of The Chicago Banker:

It probably will require a movie fan strike to bring Hollywood to a sense of decency? The public can have decent pictures and respectable private life in Hollywood if it will insist upon reform.

The ten "Fatty" Arbuckle jurors who voted to convict were gentiles. Write your own ticket.

Epilogue

[*The Seattle Star*, September 17, 1921]

Mourns
Sends Dead Girl 1000 Tiger Lilies

(Los Angeles, Sept. 17.) A floral tribute of one thousand tiger lilies today lying next to the casket of Miss Virginia Rappe, as a result of whose death Roscoe Arbuckle, comedian, was charged with murder.

It was the offering of Henry Lehrman of New York, Miss Rappe's fiancé, who wired, "She died fighting a woman's battle."

"To my brave sweetheart, From Henry" read Lehrman's card on the floral piece.

Miss Rappe's body arrived here from San Francisco early today for burial at Hollywood.

Lehrman mourned, but not for long. The caption to the above May 19, 1922 *Washington Times* photo read: Honeymooning with his bride, Henry Lehrman, motion picture producer, is giving little thought to "Fatty" Arbuckle these days. Last fall, when Lehrman, who was engaged to Virginia Rappe, heard of her death, he could find no words strong enough to denounce Arbuckle. He threatened to kill "Fatty" if the latter were freed. But since Henry wedded Miss Jocelyn Leign he doesn't care a rap about Arbuckle.

[*Great Falls Tribune*, April 13, 1922]
Arbuckle Picture to Test Public Feeling Shortly
(New York, April 12.) One of Roscoe C. (Fatty) Arbuckle's comedy drama pictures will be released within 30 days in a test of public opinion, it was announced Wednesday night, by Adolph Zukor[25], president of the Famous Players-Lasky Corporation, when informed of the comedian's acquittal.

"As to Mr. Arbuckle's future activity in motion pictures, it may be said to depend on the attitude of his public," Mr. Zukor said. "We will release one of his pictures within the next 30 days for the purpose of gauging public sentiment. If the picture meets with favorable reception, we will release others. We will not force the pictures, but will supply them as public demand exists.

"Mr. Arbuckle will not act for the present."

Four years later:

[*Evening Star*, March 19, 1926]
Arbuckle in Film Post
Banished Movie Comedian Restored to Screen Work
(Hollywood, Calif., March 19.) Roscoe Arbuckle, one time famous film comedian, has been signed by Metro-Goldwyn-Mayer to direct Marian Davies' next picture, officers of the producing company said yesterday.

Since his banishment from the screen following his trial in 1921 in connection with the death of Virginia

---

[25] Zukor was a movie mogul who later founded Paramount Pictures.

Rappe, in San Francisco, <u>Arbuckle has been directing comedies, but always under a name other than his own</u>. For the last year, he has been working for Educational Pictures.

Although acquitted in his trial, Arbuckle's name has not since that time appeared in connection with motion pictures.

[*Evening Star*, March 15, 1927]

Arbuckle Back in films
Banned Comedian Reported Signed $2,500,000 Contract

(Los Angeles, March 15.) The *Examiner* says Roscoe C. Arbuckle, whose career as a film comedian was cut short in 1921 when he was accused of responsibility for the death of Virginia Rappe, picture actress, but later acquitted, will again cavort behind the camera.

The rotund fun maker yesterday signed a contract to produce a series of comedies for Abe Carlos, independent producer, over a period of five years, which, it is said, he expects it will net him $2,500,000.

All of the pictures will be made abroad. They will be distributed in England, France, Germany and other foreign countries. Carlos plans later to bring them to the United States.

Six years later: Reportedly, Arbuckle signed a film contract to mark his triumphant return to the screen in 1933; that night the comedian suffered a fatal heart attack, dying at the age of 46.

It doesn't seem fair to the memory of Virginia Rappe to end on a "Fatty" note.
Your editor prefers to leave the reader with this tender profile:

[*The Seattle Star*, September 17, 1921]
Life Appealed To Beautiful Virginia, Dead Film Actress

Just a glimpse of a flare-skirted jacket, snug fitting to the waist, a tailored pair of riding breeches drab colored silk encasing shapely legs – high black VICI-kid[26] riding boots and a small jockey's cap with a long visor to protect the eyes.

How many residents of Hollywood have seen the familiar figure of a beautiful brunette girl – just emerging from extreme youth, dressed as above, headed for a hike in the hills.

"Isn't she a beauty?" Many a person would exclaim as Virginia Rappe – with her raven tresses pulled back boyishly from her forehead – would look up from under the peaked cap.

Even among the pretty girls of the motion picture colony, Virginia's striking exquisiteness stood out above the average.

Maybe she'd meet a friend.

"Off for a hike, Virginia?" Would be a form of salutation.

"My dear, I'm reducing," would be the rejoinder in mock dismay.

Her svelte figure, supple as a child of 10, swaying with the grace of youth, in her formfitting clothes and

---

[26] A popular brand of leather boots.

stout walking boots, would give a humorous touch to her remark.

If Virginia were trying to cut down weight, she was enough of the eternal feminine to keep the tragic truth to herself! <u>Her constant companion would be with her – Jeff! Jeff is one of those big, plainspoken dogs</u> – and when he talked, he meant business. Anyone wanting to bother Virginia with talk first to her representative Jeff.

But Virginia will never hike again.

The modish flare skirted jacket; the pair of tailored riding breeches of drab colored silk – her riding boots are but a few of the remaining evidences that Virginia was a vivacious, warm-blooded young girl just a few short days ago!

And how she was interested in life – in everything!

One day it would be motoring – then perhaps ocean bathing would be the absorbing interest in her existence – then the sewing or cooking bug would devour her entire being.

Virginia Rappe was an average girl – with normal desires – and fits of impulsiveness that controlled maidens.

"Why, I saw her only three days before they started for San Francisco," said Miss Helen Hansen, 1053 North Oxford Ave., another screen actress – referring to the weekend trip to San Francisco which resulted in the death of Virginia Rappe. "Al Semnacher had asked me to go and Virginia seemed insistent."

Miss Hansen was stunned by the report of the girl's tragic end – and the unfortunate incidents surrounding it.

"I was making some *crepe de chine* underthings, and Virginia was so interested in how I was making them! You know, she couldn't do anything like that, but she wanted to learn – she was just determined to learn how!

"So in the afternoon she came over and we cut out a lot of stuff, but she made such a botch of it, and finally she became disgusted and threw it aside."

She was never known to mention "Fatty" Arbuckle – the man held in San Francisco for murder, among her friends.

"I think the only man she cared anything in the world about was Henry Lehrman," the chum continued. "She was awfully fond of him and kept wishing that he would hurry back from New York."

He was never out of the girl's thoughts, the actress maintained. "You know how girls will talk," the moving picture girl put it, "but during all our conversations she has never mentioned liking another man – even casually.

"She was a girl who didn't go around much. In fact, I never knew of her being at a party and I'm pretty certain she never went out with another man.

"Except that Mrs. Delmont and Semnacher's son were going, I don't think she would have gone on that trip north."

Mrs. Joseph Hardebeck, 504 North Wilton Pl., who stood in the relation of a foster mother to the dead girl, also says that Arbuckle was an unknown quantity in the young actress' life.

"She never mentioned his name except in connection with his pictures, and no one who knew her could picture her receiving the attentions of this man," said Mrs. Hardebeck, who professed herself completely mystified by Arbuckle's reported remark to Miss Rappe, "I've been waiting five years to get you."

"Mr. Arbuckle never came to the house to see her," asserted the girl's foster mother. "I am certain he never made any advances, and if he had any designs on her she didn't know it."

<u>Such was Virginia Rappe's character that any low or common act was impossible to her</u>, according to Mrs. Hardebeck, with whom she had lived since the death of her mother 13 years ago. From the time of her mother's death she remained a girl of 18 in disposition and spirit, said "aunty."

Virginia Rappe and "Jeff." *The Evening Herald* reported that Jeff "wanders aimlessly about the bungalow in Hollywood where Miss Rappe used to live, refusing to eat or to be consoled."

Forty Quarts of Liquor

Bamber Books
facebook.com/BamberBooks

Printed in Great Britain
by Amazon